Catching the
Wind of the Spirit

Catching the Wind of the Spirit

Sunder Krishnan
with Dale Losch

WingSpread Publishers
Camp Hill, Pennsylvania

WingSpread Publishers
Camp Hill, Pennsylvania
www.wingspreadpublishers.com

A division of Zur Ltd.

Catching the Wind of the Spirit
ISBN: 978-1-60066-272-0
LOC Control Number: 2010938399
© 2010 by Sunder Krishnan
Chapter 9 © 2010 by Dale Losch

14 13 12 11 10   5 4 3 2 1

Cover design by Pencil Tip Design

Also by Sunder Krishnan:
The Conquest of Inner Space
Loving God with All You've Got

Contents

Introduction

You Were Created for Conformity

In an article in the magazine *Leadership*, pastor and author John Ortberg observes that as Christians today, we too often find ourselves laboring under the mistaken notion that our life of faith here on earth is little more than an interlude to our eventual transport to heaven. He writes,

> We are content with conversion when God is calling for transformation. Rather than expecting the kingdom of God to revolutionize lives today, we hope it will happen in heaven tomorrow. Somewhere along the line we swapped out Jesus' gospel—through Him we can be transformed into citizens of the kingdom of God right now, today—for a gospel of heaven's minimum entrance requirement.[1]

Our True Purpose

How different this idea is from the true design of the gospel that we see in Scripture. It is an idea that has limited many of God's people to a level of faith and spiritual maturity far below their true calling. In reality, there is a more fundamental and glorious purpose for our salvation than merely making it to heaven when our life on earth is complete. In Romans 8:29 the Apostle Paul explains that from the very beginning God's plan was to "shape the lives of those who love him along the same lines as the life of his Son. The Son stands first in the line of humanity he restored. We see the original and intended shape of our lives there in him" (*The Message*).

In other words, we have been redeemed in order to be progressively transformed into the likeness of Christ. However, this transformation does not boil down to mere external conformity or the imitation of certain "Christlike" actions or lifestyles. Rather, it is a continuous, ongoing transformation of the inner person, so that the inward change (being conformed to the image of Christ) dramatically impacts our outward person (our motives, attitudes, words and actions).

As a pastor, I consider it one of my primary responsibilities to encourage believers in this process of personal transformation into the likeness of Christ. And like the Apostle Paul as he ministered to the church at Galatia, the intensity of this responsibility should be like the "pains of childbirth" (Galatians 4:19) as I attempt to labor in prayer and the Word to see Christ formed in those individuals to whom God has personally called me to minister.

Christ's Birth in Us

I want to take this birthing analogy a step further as we explore the process of being conformed to Christ's image, because it is crucial to understand that this transformation has nothing to do with some sort of self-improvement program, or a set of activities that we must add to our already busy lives and packed schedules. In fact, it is from beginning to end a work of God's Holy Spirit in us, and in the story of how Mary bore the precious Son of God, I think that we can get an inspired picture of Christ being formed within each of us.

Consider that Mary was the only human being in whom Jesus was physically formed, and that formation came as the power of the Holy Spirit overshadowed Mary. For the next nine months her body was literally shaped and formed as the Christ child grew within her. But that formation and shaping didn't stop when Mary delivered Jesus and laid Him in the manger in Bethlehem. It continued deep within her heart as she quietly, attentively observed the one and only Son of God growing "in wisdom and stature, and in favor with God and men" (Luke 2:52).

The Apostle Paul writes of a similar working of the Holy Spirit as we come to faith and Christ begins to be formed in us:

> A new power is in operation. The Spirit of life in Christ, like a strong wind, has magnificently cleared the air, freeing you from a fated lifetime of brutal tyranny at the hands of sin and death. . . . And now what the law code asked for but we couldn't deliver is accomplished as we, instead of redoubling our own

efforts, simply embrace what the Spirit is doing in us. (Romans 8:2, 4, *The Message*)

A Cooperative Effort

It is through the overshadowing and controlling power of the Holy Spirit that we are redeemed and Christ is formed in us. But just because it is the work of the Holy Spirit does not mean we have no part in this process of transformation. It is a cooperative work, and I don't know of a better analogy to illustrate this than the example I once read[2] of three different water vessels: a rowboat, a raft and a sailboat.

The propulsion of a rowboat requires someone in the boat to pick up the two oars and put a significant amount of effort into moving the boat through the water. Without that person rowing, the boat will go nowhere. A raft, on the other hand, requires no effort at all from its passengers. They can sit and do nothing, while the waves propel the vessel along. Unfortunately, because the raft lacks any effective means for steering the craft, its passengers find themselves completely at the mercy of the waves for whatever random direction they might find themselves headed. In fact, they might find themselves moving in the opposite direction than they wish to go, or if they are caught in an eddy, their hapless raft might even be capsized by the force of the elements around them.

Unlike these first two vessels, a sailboat relies on both the force of the wind and the skill of its pilot for successful navigation. The pilot supplies no power at all to propel the vessel forward. That comes from the wind. But if the pilot does not hoist the sails and position them properly, that readily available wind will never be harnessed to steer the vessel's chosen course.

The wind and the sailboat are a picture of the cooperation between the Holy Spirit and the willing believer who seeks to be transformed into the likeness of Christ. That is why I have entitled this book *Catching the Wind of the Spirit*. It is the Spirit of God who performs this vital work of progressively transforming each of us into the image of our Savior and Lord. But in order to be effectively steered and directed by the Spirit, it is important for us to embrace the handful of spiritual disciplines that we will discuss in this book: worship, Scripture meditation and study, prayer, confession, fellowship, service and giving. They are, if you will, the sails that will manifestly aid us in steering our course toward conformity to Christ's image.[3]

A Word of Warning

Perhaps you are reading these pages and find yourself thinking, *I'm not really sure I am all that interested in this journey you're talking about. I'm honestly not certain I want to embrace worship, the Word, prayer, fellowship with other believers, spiritual service and giving. I just don't know how much I want to commit to being totally transformed into Christ's image. What if I am actually content with heaven's minimum entrance requirements?*

If this is an honest appraisal of your feelings, you are certainly not alone. In a survey a few years back, Christian researcher George Barna found that there are an estimated forty-five million individuals in North America who claim to be born again based on two basic convictions: They believe that a personal commitment to

Jesus Christ is important, and they believe they are going to heaven because they have confessed their sins and received Him as Savior. In other words, they have satisfied what they believe are heaven's minimum entrance requirements. But Barna's survey also found that the lifestyles and values of the majority (about 66 percent) of these "born again" individuals are really not much different from those who claim no faith in Christ.[4]

If you find yourself among this grouping of people who call themselves Christians but whose lives don't clearly reflect the character of Christ, then I must confront you with a sobering possibility: Perhaps you need to take a very close look at your spiritual condition. Is it possible that you really aren't born again after all? Please hear me out.

A Radical Change

Scripture is clear that those who are truly born again through faith in Christ will experience a radical change in their lives. While we could spend several pages citing chapter and verse, just one book, John's First Epistle, offers overwhelming evidence of the dramatic transformation that we can expect from those who have truly been redeemed through faith in Jesus Christ:

- They are freed from the habit and bondage of sin (3:6; 5:18).

- They have overcome their love (and lust) for the things of this world (2:15–16).

- They are seeking daily to know and love God, to keep His Word, and to live in a Christlike manner (2:3–6).

• They have an active love for others, and seek for ways to serve as God's hands extended to those around them (2:9–11, 3:16–18).

Jesus declares that "no one can see the kingdom of God unless he is born again" (John 3:3), and much of the rest of the New Testament offers clear evidence of the changes that will occur in those who are truly born again. Thus, the logic of Scripture ruthlessly demonstrates that if you consider yourself a born-again Christian and yet you are not finding yourself progressively, consistently being transformed into the likeness of Christ—nor, indeed, do you have any great desire for such a transformation—then there is a distinct possibility that you have never been truly born again of the Spirit of God.

Taking the First Step

This book is all about taking us beyond this false notion that there is a "minimum entrance requirement" that is sufficient to get us into heaven and exploring how each one of us can move effectively from the new birth to spiritual maturity, which is nothing less than being conformed to the image and nature of Christ.

However, just as it is not possible for a child to grow inside a woman's womb without conception taking place first, it is absolutely impossible for anyone to catch the wind of the Spirit and grow in the likeness of Christ without first being truly redeemed through faith in Christ.

That's the place to begin.

Acknowledgements

Even a modest project like this is made possible by the glad and competent cooperation of many individuals. I am indebted to:

- the congregation of Rexdale Alliance Church, who first heard this material in a sermon series and whose enthusiastic feedback and endorsement gave me some hope that the material would indeed prove helpful to others;

- two editors, David Bohon and Dave Fessenden, who turned my awkward prose into fluid and readable material;

- Pamela Brossman, for her patience with me when I missed deadlines and needed grace;

- Ken Paton, for his vision and commitment to make sound yet simple biblical exegesis from a pastoral perspective accessible to laypeople who are neither pastors nor exegetes, nor have the time or inclination to wade through scholarly tomes.

During the last few years God has seen fit to forge strong links of compassion between several individuals in our church and the country of Cambodia. Under the gifted and passionate leadership of one individual, several have invested prayer and presence to advocate on behalf of vulnerable young boys and girls caught in the maws of the ruthless sex-slave trade. It is my joy to dedicate this book to these advocates who will not let our congregation forget Isaiah's injunction to seek justice.

Chapter 1

Regenerated by the Spirit

What comes to your mind when you think of Simon Peter, the great servant of God who figures so prominently in much of New Testament Scripture? A simple fisherman whom Jesus called to be a "fisher of men"? A brash and bold disciple of Christ who was infinitely zealous but lacking in vital discipline? A fearful coward who denied Christ and ran away? Or a humble man of God who, filled with the Holy Spirit on the Day of Pentecost, rose to become one of the early church's chief spokesmen and apostles?

Of course, typically when we consider the life of Peter, we don't think of who he was, but who he became. We think of him as the Apostle Peter, whom God used mightily to establish the early church, and who laid down everything—including, ultimately, his life—because of his love for the Lord Jesus Christ.

But it is crucial for us to understand that for this to occur—for Peter, the lowly and humble fisherman to become the bold, uncompromising spokesman and leader in the early church—required a massive change of identity, a transformation that happened when he first met Jesus at the Lake of Gennesaret. The account we find in Luke 5 of this first meeting is so familiar that I think there is a tendency for us to miss the enormity of what happened to Peter and how it mirrors what happens to each of us when we come to faith in Christ. For it was not just the moment that Peter discovered his life's vocation—it was also the moment that he realized his sinful condition and his need for a total transformation.

Responding to Christ's Call

The scene here is a typical one for Jesus. He is speaking the Word of God with matchless authority and power, and needy people weighed down with the cares of life are drawn to Him in a dramatic way. The crowd grows so large that Jesus finds He must co-opt one of the fishing boats by the water where He is standing—a boat belonging to Peter, a local fisherman. Turning to this rough and rugged workingman, who is no doubt a little distracted following a long and fruitless night of labor at his nets, Jesus directs Peter to push the boat out from the shore a little, and He continues to preach.

Even as He gives His undivided focus to the crowd, listening with rapt attention to every word He speaks, Christ has by no means forgotten about Peter, whom I can picture standing in the background taking in this scene with a detached reserve. In fact, this is no mere chance encounter between the Messiah and the fisherman, but a divine appointment written on God's timetable from the foundation of the world. As Jesus concludes His ministry to the crowd, He purposely turns to Peter and directs him:

> "Put out into deep water, and let down the nets for a catch."
>
> Simon answered, "Master, we've worked hard all night and haven't caught anything. But because you say so, I will let down the nets."
>
> When they had done so, they caught such a large number of fish that their nets began to break. So they signaled their partners in the other boat to come and help them, and they came and filled both boats so full that they began to sink.
>
> When Simon Peter saw this, he fell at Jesus' knees and said, "Go away from me, Lord; I am a sinful man!" For he and all his companions were astonished at the catch of fish they had taken, and so were James and John, the sons of Zebedee, Simon's partners.
>
> Then Jesus said to Simon, "Don't be afraid; from now on you will catch men." So they pulled their boats up on shore, left everything and followed him. (Luke 5:4–11)

A Predictable Life

Now, this is a pretty straightforward story, so simple a child can understand the surface implications: Jesus calls Simon Peter, a fisherman, to be His disciple and to become a "fisher of men"—preaching the Word of God like Peter had just observed Jesus doing. But if that is as far as we take this story, we have missed a crucial element that is key to the transformation God desires for each one of us. Let's take a closer look at this account and see where it is actually taking this future servant of God.

Christ's first encounter with Peter occurs following a long night that found Peter and his companions diligently plying their trade as fishermen on Lake Gennesaret—and catching nothing. Now as discouraging as that might seem, you fishermen can confirm that coming up empty is not an unheard-of occurrence after a long day (or night) on the water. It just comes with the territory. For Simon Peter, who made his livelihood as a fisherman, I am sure it was something he expected from time to time. After years spent fishing on a body of water he probably knew like the back of his hand, experiencing a lean day now and then was something that probably didn't upset the pace of his life all that much.

Day in and day out, he and his companions were accustomed to sailing the length and breadth of this long and wide freshwater lake, casting their nets in the areas where they knew schools of tilapia and other native species congregated. Each morning, after a long night on the water, they would clean their catch, take it to the busy marketplace to sell, wash and mend their nets and equipment and prepare for another night of fishing.

This was the life Peter knew and a life his father and grandfather before him probably practiced as well. No doubt it was a hard life, a rigorous life, but it was also wellordered and predictable—and more than anything else it defined who Peter was. Peter was a fisherman; that was his identity, as well as that of his companions. Unlike many of us today, it is unlikely that Peter had much time or inclination to ponder such ethereal concerns as, "Who am I?" or "Where am I going?" As far as he was concerned, he was a fisherman and that was all he would ever be.

A Change of Identity

But that day something monumental was about to happen that would dramatically change what Peter thought about who he was—and who he was to become. After he and his fellow fishermen had labored fruitlessly over their nets the entire night, Jesus turns to Peter and says with the authority of the One who had created the lake and the fish that dwelt in its depths, "Put out into deep water, and let down the nets for a catch."

Now think about it: This is a rabbi and a carpenter telling a man whose whole identity is wrapped up in being a fisherman how to do his job. In fact, He is telling him to do something that years of experience told Peter would be an exercise in futility. Peter was probably thinking, *Rabbi, why don't you stick to the synagogue or making yokes? Who are you to tell me how to fish when I have just labored all night?* What we know of Peter's boldness would indicate that he probably had to hold his tongue. Instead, out of respect for Jesus' reputation as a rabbi—a teacher—he concedes, "Master, we've worked hard all night and haven't caught anything. But because you say so, I will let down the nets."

And with that subtle concession, Peter's life is suddenly invaded by the miraculous power of the Lord Jesus Christ. He goes from laboring all night and having no fish, to obeying an illogical request from a rabbi he just met and being faced with a professional emergency: so many fish that his nets are breaking and his boat is sinking.

You can probably imagine Peter's amazement and excitement as he instantaneously receives a harvest such as he had never experienced in his whole life. "Wow, what a catch!" he must have yelled to his fellow fishermen as their nets strained and they filled their boats with more fish—and income—than they had probably ever seen at one time. "We're going to have a good day in the marketplace today!"

But in the midst of all the laughter, excitement and amazement, Peter is suddenly struck with the reality of what he is experiencing. *Wait a minute!* he must have thought. *We just spent a whole night in these very waters and caught nothing. Where did all these fish come from?*

For a Jew living in Israel, there could be only one answer to that question. It was the sovereign Lord, the Maker of heaven and the earth, who did this thing. This man who had told Peter to let down his nets was no mere rabbi. Peter is suddenly struck with the undeniable sense that he is in the presence of someone much greater than a teacher. And with that thought comes a much more terrifying realization for Peter, one that brings him to his knees before Jesus with this desperate confession: "Lord, I am a sinner! Go away from me!"

In that one instant, Simon Peter's identity is changed. He is no longer a fisherman who had a bad day. Nor does he see himself as an okay guy who is a little rough around the edges. He doesn't try to justify who he is before this man who has just performed an incredible miracle. No, everything is suddenly changed in his life, and he is reduced to one core identity: "I am a sinner." And because he has now been totally exposed as a sinner, there is only one thing that he can do—get as far away from Jesus as possible. While he probably isn't sure how he knows, Peter is sure that the man standing there before him has a direct connection to the holy and righteous God of Israel, and his response is the same as that of the prophet Isaiah when he was brought face-to-face with almighty God: "Woe to me! . . . I am ruined! For I am a man of unclean lips, and I live among a people of unclean lips, and my eyes have seen the King, the LORD Almighty" (Isaiah 6:5).

Christ Responds in Mercy

Jesus' response to Peter's fear and self-loathing is immediate and decisive: "Don't be afraid." Yes, Peter is rightly fearful at this divine encounter that takes him far beyond his comfortable identity as a fisherman and brings him to his core identity as a sinner. Let's also consider, for a moment, the things that Jesus does not say to Peter—the things that so many people today confronted by their own sinfulness are accustomed to hearing from pastors, spiritual advisers, therapists and counselors. Jesus *doesn't* respond to Peter's confession by telling him, "Forget all this sinner business; you're a good guy. Don't you know all the potential there is within you? Everyone is created in the image of God, so get up off your knees and stop beating yourself up! You're okay." No, Jesus is well aware of Peter's sinfulness. Ridding Peter of the sin problem is the reason He came to earth.

Notice, also, that Jesus *doesn't* say, "Yeah, Peter, you're a sinner, and that's a big problem." He knows Peter's condition, and it has just become a revelation to Peter himself. Jesus didn't come to point out the obvious—that humanity is lost in sin and condemned to eternal death.

Speaking of Himself, Jesus says that "God did not send his Son into the world to condemn the world, but to save the world through him" (John 3:17). Elsewhere He declares that His purpose in coming to earth was so that you and I "may have life, and have it to the full" (John 10:10).

Once Peter has been reduced to an understanding of his core identity as a sinner before a holy God, Jesus immediately thrusts him into a new life and a new identity, telling him in effect, "Peter, from now on you are going to catch men, just like you have spent so many years on this lake catching fish. Only now your labor will be for the souls of humanity. I am calling you to a higher identity, one I will create and confirm in you." And with that, Peter is converted to Christ, abandons his old life and embraces the new.

So often in our Western culture, we equate conversion to Christ with certain actions people take, like coming down to the altar at church and saying a sinner's prayer. Believe me, I am not against those things because I know that countless individuals have come to faith in Christ in just those ways. But if Peter's experience isn't a conversion to faith in Christ, I don't know what is. It is as clear a picture as you will find of what it means to be born again by the Spirit of God. His "sinner's prayer" was fervent, effectual and from the heart: "Go away from me, Lord; I am a sinful man!"

Jesus came close instead—and changed Peter for time and eternity.

Four Crucial Steps to Conversion

Now, because each of us is unique, and because the Holy Spirit is infinitely creative, the redemptive process is never a canned business. It never happens in exactly the same way for each person. He will not speak to an engineer, a chemist, a doctor or an attorney in just the same way He speaks to a truck driver, a farmer, a housewife, a teenager or a rock star. Each conversion story will be different and profound in its own unique way. Nevertheless, the story of Peter's encounter with Christ suggests four indispensable elements that will be present if that conversion to Christ is to be genuine. Let's take a close look at each one.

Divine initiative. In looking at this account, it is clear that everything that happened to Peter that day happened because of Jesus' initiative. Jesus showed up right where Peter was and chose his boat. Jesus got into that boat and directed Peter to push it out into the water. Jesus told Peter to drop his nets where Peter was certain there would be no fish, and the resulting catch, as Jesus knew it would be, was more than Peter and his friends could handle. While it is true that Peter had to respond to Jesus, it was Jesus who first reached out to Peter.

In John 3:3, the New International Version of the Bible has Jesus declaring that "no one can see the kingdom of God unless he is born again." But if we look at the original words in the Greek, what Jesus is actually saying is that we must be born "from above." There is a profound, unalterable truth in those words: Salvation through Christ is something that happens from outside of you and not something that you generate. It happens by God's own initiative, through His Holy Spirit.

Most often this divine initiative happens through the written or proclaimed Word of God. It might happen as someone is listening to the Word of God preached in a sermon or during an evangelistic meeting. How many millions of individuals have come to Christ as they have listened to Billy Graham preaching the Word of God in a stadium, over the television or on a radio program?

Likewise, countless millions of individuals throughout the ages have come to a saving knowledge of Christ as they have read the Bible in their homes, in hotel rooms, in college dormitories or even in prison cells, to name just a few places. Even Scripture read from scraps of paper have been the divine initiative leading people to Christ. I once read the story of a man who used the pages from a Bible as paper to roll his own cigarettes. He managed to smoke his way through the Gospels of Matthew, Mark and Luke, but by the time he made it to the Gospel of John, God had gotten hold of his heart, and he was converted.

Miraculously, there are even people all over the world who hear the Word of God through Jesus coming to them in dreams. Now, that's what I call divine initiative.

A realization of who Jesus really is. Many people consider Jesus to be a great teacher, prophet, spiritual leader or the wisest man who ever lived. Yes, He was all of those things, but acknowledging Him as such is not enough. It is only the realization that He is the sovereign Holy Lord of creation that will lead an individual to new birth. And that can only come by revelation of the Holy Spirit. As Peter struggled over the nets filled with fish that day on the Lake of Gennesaret, he was suddenly confronted with the reality that standing before him was God in human form, and that led him to the next realization.

A realization of our core identity before Christ.
As Peter stood before Jesus, he knew beyond a shadow of a doubt that he was a sinner in need of mercy. The same realization must confront each of us before we can truly be born "from above." We must move beyond the humanistic notion that we are reasonably decent people, or that at least we are better than that pathetic, twice-divorced man who lives down the street or those unfortunate individuals living in the homeless shelter downtown. That realization will come with the recognition of our desperate need for mercy and grace—apart from which we have no hope of salvation.

Forget about meeting heaven's minimum entrance requirement; you and I can't even meet the first iota of God's requirement because infinite holiness demands infinite perfection. Mercy and grace are our only hope, and it is the Holy Spirit who opens our eyes to this eternal truth.

A response of faith that follows Jesus to progressively realize our new identity.
The capacity to believe is a gift that God gives to us. The Apostle Paul makes this clear when he declares that "it is by grace you have been saved, through faith—and this not from yourselves, it is the gift of God—not by works, so that no one can boast" (Ephesians 2:8–9). With this response of faith there comes a radical change in the direction of our lives and in our identities. As Peter responded in faith and

received this new identity from Christ, Scripture tells us that he pulled his boat to shore, "left everything" and followed Christ. No longer would he identify himself as a fisherman—or a sinner!

Likewise, true conversion for you and me results in a similar abandon in our own lives, as we make a conscious spiritual decision to lay down everything else in life—our sin, our past, our ambitions, our goals, our futures—and submit all to the lordship of Christ.

My Own Birth from Above

It is impossible for me to write about the new birth in Christ without thinking back to my own conversion. God's initiative in my life began on January 11, 1963, when for the first time I heard the gospel. While not a lot happened right away, for the first time I read the Bible and began to understand, not the religion known as Christianity, but who Jesus was and the claims He has made on my life.

That was the first step, and it took until May 21, 1963, for the next two steps to occur, when after hearing the gospel during a meeting at summer camp I responded to the altar call. Now, I tend to respond to things in a rational rather than an emotional way. But I can tell you that day, no sooner was the altar call given than my heart began thumping inexplicably, and as I went forward, knelt and joined in the simple chorus "My Jesus I Love Thee," the tears began to flow. I didn't know it then, but the Holy Spirit was doing the work of regeneration, and I clearly understood that I was a sinner desperately in need of mercy before a holy God.

Now after my conversion, Jesus didn't immediately

direct me to leave the "nets" that I had in my hands at the time. So I continued the educational track I was on, studying engineering for the next six years in India and the United States, and then went to work as a nuclear engineer in Canada. It wasn't until October 1980 that Jesus opened the door for me to lay down my nets as an engineer, pick up a new set of nets and join the pastoral staff of Rexdale Alliance Church in Toronto, Ontario, Canada, where I have served the past thirty years.

Where Are You?

As you are reading these pages, you might have come to the realization that all is not right in your own relationship with God. Perhaps you have repeated a sinner's prayer and even gone through all the right motions, but looking at where you are today, at the condition of your heart, you would have to acknowledge, "I really have not been born from above by the Spirit of God."

My prayer is that you will respond to His divine initiative (do you wonder why you are reading this book at this time?), acknowledge that Jesus truly is God made flesh, make the declaration as Peter did, "I am a sinner," trust Jesus to grant you a new identity and allow Him to begin the process of transforming you into His own image. If you are banking on some prayer you repeated once, if you are counting on the power of a Christian heritage and tradition or if you are relying on certain "Christian" behaviors like going to church, reading the Bible, praying and giving a little bit of money in the offering plate, then you have traded the true gospel that will lead you into the likeness of Christ for a false gospel that cannot save you.

Not Perfection, but Direction

On the other hand, you might be a true child of God, but because of your particular life circumstances, you feel constrained to confess, "I am not as enthusiastic as I should be about embracing this journey of progressive transformation into Christlikeness." Identifying these indispensable elements of true conversion might have only served to pour guilt on your troubled conscience.

If you identify with those sentiments, remember this: What matters is not perfection but the direction you are moving in. Consider a very different kind of conversion that I experienced in May of 2000, when I came back after a speaking engagement in Hong Kong with my very first single lens reflex (SLR) camera in hand. Before that I was one of the millions of casual "point and shoot" photographers armed with an elementary compact camera. At family gatherings, mostly, I would literally point and shoot with no particular thought to composition, lighting, depth of field, etc. I would get the film developed, put the photos in an album and forgot about them.

But the SLR purchase in Hong Kong changed all that. As I began to read about what these cameras could do, I was gripped by the technical aspects of my new camera. That led me to read books by professional photographers aimed at helping people like me get to the next level of proficiency. I went to Web sites and read comments about peoples' photographs and what made them good or bad. I looked at my own "bad" photographs and learned why they were bad and stopped repeating those mistakes. I also learned how to make them good the next time I shot a similar subject. At the weddings that I officiated, I picked up tips from the professional photographer hired for the event, asking questions about the equipment he/she used, how he/she handled backlighting, etc. I upgraded my digital image processing software.

I had been a photographer before—there was no question about that. I had just stagnated and was now moving again—to new heights and joys. So too with your spiritual life. Let Peter's encounter with Christ awaken you, not to the experience of new birth, but to new "SLR levels" of the life of Christ in you, stagnated though it might be at a "point and shoot" stage. The following chapters are the "photography manuals" to help you on the journey.

Questions for Group Study

1. Have someone read Luke 5:4–11. Without referring back to the chapter, see if you can identify the four steps to conversion that the author draws out of this passage. Do you agree that this incident was the point of Peter's conversion? Why or why not?

2. Peter was converted because Jesus took the initiative. Can you identify an incident in your life as well where God took the initiative to lead you to Himself? Share that story.

3. Peter was converted because he realized who Jesus really is—the sovereign Lord. Think back on your life. Can you name a point at which you came to a realization of Jesus' true identity?

4. Peter was converted because he realized who he really was—a sinner. Share a time when you became aware of your need for a Savior.

5. Peter was converted because he responded in faith. Do you have a story to share about how you "left your nets" to follow Christ?

6. Take some time to take an honest spiritual inventory and determine if you are truly converted, and if not, ask God to lead you to a place of salvation. If you can say that you are truly converted but your spiritual fervor has been allowed to decline, ask God for His power and enabling and pray that He will lead you to others who will encourage you in your new walk of faith. Perhaps as a group, you can commit to provide that spiritual encouragement to one another.

Chapter 2

Worship:
Reflecting His Glory

One Sunday in the mid-nineteenth century, the great American orator Henry Ward Beecher was absent from his pulpit, and his less flamboyant younger brother filled in for him. Beecher's popularity was at its height, and the church was packed with a throng of worshipers expecting to hear a rousing sermon from the renowned abolitionist. So when his rather unassuming brother stepped into the pulpit instead, more than a few disappointed members of the audience began to make their way toward the exits.

But the speaker that day was thinking just a little more quickly than the departing congregants and rising rapidly he loudly declared, "All who have come here today to worship Henry Ward Beecher are free to leave. All who have come to worship God, keep your seats!"

Linking true worship to the presence or absence of a

gifted speaker is but one of the many ways we get worship wrong. It is absolutely crucial that we get it right
because worship is perhaps the most foundational of
the spiritual disciplines. We would not be stretching
the point if we were to say that all the other disciplines
addressed in this book—Scripture meditation and study,
prayer, confession, fellowship, service and giving—are
subsets of this one overarching spiritual discipline of
worship.

Redeemed to Worship

Scripture emphatically states that God not only created but redeemed us to worship Him. In the Exodus
account of God's deliverance of His people Israel from
bondage in Egypt, we have a front-row seat as we witness the magnificent display of His power, culminating
in His miraculous leading of Israel through the dry
land of the parted Red Sea and of His destruction of the
Egyptian forces when they tried to follow. Three times
in Exodus God declares, "I will gain glory for myself
because of what will happen to Pharaoh and his whole
army" (14:4, NIRV; see also 14:17–18). The manner of
the redemption of His people was to incite worship, to
demonstrate His glory.

He quickly followed up this magnificent deliverance
by giving Israel specific instruction on how they were to
worship Him: "in the splendor of his holiness" (Psalm
29:2). From the setting up of the tabernacle to the establishing of the priestly order, to the minute details of how
they were to relate to Him, God ensured that the people
He had redeemed and delivered from the hand of the

enemy would continue to engage in the promotion of
His glory through a lifestyle of worship.

As with the Old, so it is with the New Testament.
Look, for example, at just the first fourteen verses of
Ephesians 1, where the Apostle Paul absolutely ransacks
the vocabulary of the original Greek to demonstrate for
us the riches of this thing called redemption and the
worship that is to be our response. In verses 5 and 6 he
explains that God "predestined us to be adopted as his
sons through Jesus Christ, in accordance with his pleasure and will—*to the praise of his glorious grace.*"

In verses 11 and 12 he writes that we were chosen
and redeemed so that we might be *"for the praise of his
glory."* And again in verses 13 and 14, he explains that
God sealed our redemption with the guarantee of His
Holy Spirit, *"to the praise of his glory."*

Finally, with the last book of the Bible, Revelation,
we witness the consummation of history and redemption, with "a great multitude that no one could count,
from every nation, tribe, people and language, standing before the throne and in front of the Lamb" (7:9),
ascribing to Him glory, honor and power and dominion
and majesty and worth forever and ever.

Our Need, Not His

So from the beginning of Genesis to the end of Revelation, you come to the inescapable conclusion that God
created us—and redeemed us—to worship Him. Now
this immediately raises an important question. If God
redeemed us for His glory and commands us to praise
Him, does this mean that God is the supreme egotist?
After all, we know from human experience that we are

naturally repelled by the arrogance of any individual who demands exaltation and adoration—whether he is a pastor who thinks the church exists for him, or a CEO who expects his employees to exalt him.

But is it the same when the Creator of the universe demands our worship and expects our focus to be only upon Him? This is a crucial question to which we need a definitive answer if we are to move into a serious engagement in worship. And to find the answer, we must begin with the fundamental difference between God and us.

As human beings, you and I are creatures of need; we thrive on esteem and affirmation, and our spirits tend to wither when we are ignored or denigrated. But God, because He is God, has nothing in Him that corresponds to human need. Unlike us, He is self-existent and totally self-sufficient. There is, quite literally, nothing that He needs. Our worship is not going to make Him more glorious, nor is He going to lose some of His glory if we withhold our worship. So His command for us to worship Him must have something to do with how we are impacted.

In order to explore just how worship touches us, let's take a brief look at how we respond to the beauty of God's creation. During a vacation not long ago, my wife, Sham, and I traveled to Arizona where we had an opportunity to experience firsthand the red-rock beauty of Sedona. Surrounded by massive rock formations of spectacular red and orange hues, this community has become a favorite destination for tourists and sightseers. And as we drove our rented car through this picturesque area, we found ourselves exclaiming to one another, "Did you see that?" We would turn a corner and glance back at what we had just spent several minutes observing in wonder, and find ourselves completely blown away at being presented with a new and totally different perspective that was just as beautiful as what we had just seen.

On our second day of enjoying this majestic beauty, Sham turned to me and commented, "I never get tired of looking at this."

"Me neither!" I said. I had my camera with me, and I felt compelled to capture as much as I could of the seemingly endless variations of beauty that unfolded before me. I found myself desperately trying to set up different shots, first with a wide-angle lens, followed by a zoom lens, to record the majestic panorama that was triggering such a deep response within me.

By habit I am not a big risk taker, but I would park in some very risky locations in the road (much to Sham's consternation) in order to get just the right angle for an unforgettable photo. The joy I was experiencing was worth the extra effort, and even a little risk.

But what if, instead of getting in the car and making that effort to see these world-famous rock formations, Sham and I had been content to sit in our motel room and watch television all day long? While the red rocks of Sedona would not have lost one bit of their splendor, their beauty would have been lost to us. We would have lost out on a once-in-a-lifetime experience that was ready and available to us, all because we chose not to engage in it.

It is a bit of a paradox that when we encounter hugeness in creation, it simultaneously makes us feel small while enlarging our souls. Our exclamations—"Did you see that?" "Look!" "Let me stop and take a picture," "I wish I could get closer"—are all responses of adoration that are appropriate to the majesty of the object. But our response has no impact on what we are viewing. Everything that happens is inside of us.

Now let's apply this to the awe we might feel in beholding God in all His glory. He is the ultimate in grandeur and wonder, and our worship is the appropriate response of our finite human hearts to the revelation of His infinite majesty. But our worship doesn't change God one iota. It's all about what it does to us. Far from being the demand of an egocentric God who somehow feels better when humans worship Him, God's scriptural command to worship Him is an invitation for us to come into His presence and be "transformed into his likeness with ever-increasing glory" (2 Corinthians 3:18). What shape does this transformation take, you might ask?

What Happens When We Worship

Psalm 115:3–7 helps us get a handle on this:

Our God is in heaven; . . .
But their idols are silver and gold,
    made by the hands of men.
They have mouths, but cannot speak,
    eyes, but they cannot see;
they have ears, but cannot hear,
    noses, but they cannot smell;
they have hands, but cannot feel,
    feet, but they cannot walk;
    nor can they utter a sound with their throats.

There is a powerful implied contrast here between

the idols of men (which are fashioned like the men who made them but are utterly lifeless and without power) and the one true God (the living God, who has eyes that can see, ears that can hear, and so on). Then comes the critical insight that puts it all into perspective: "Those who make them will be like them, and so will all who trust in them" (115:8).

There is an important principle here that we must remember: We become like whatever we worship. When we worship that which is lifeless, something within us begins to die. We can take our admiration of the beauty of creation one step too far and worship the creature instead of the Creator. Or we can worship the living God and be gradually transformed into people with eyes that can see, ears that can hear, a mouth that can speak, and hands that are powerful to do the work of God's kingdom.

Scholars tell us that there are two Greek words for life: *bios* and *zoe*. *Bios* is the word from which we get the word "biology." It refers to the biological life that flows through each one of us. The other word, *zoe*, is more difficult to put into English, but in the New Testament context it refers to essential life, the overflowing abundant life of Christ Himself. It is the life Jesus was speaking of when He declared, "Whoever believes in me, as the Scripture has said, streams of living water will flow from within him" (John 7:38).

One of the most powerful examples of this overflowing life was the change in my father when he came to faith in Christ at the age of eighty, just three days before his death. He had spent nearly his entire life worshipping lifeless idols and by nature was a passive man who spoke very little throughout his life. One time my mother forgot to put salt in his food, but he never said a word. She didn't discover her mistake until she tasted it herself. Her obvious question, "Why didn't you say something?" brought this response: "It's all the same to me." In his later years, when he was living in our home, my children would encourage him to speak during our family devotions and his response would always be, "I don't have anything worthwhile to say."

But in those final three days of his life, he was powerfully transformed by the *zoe* life of Christ within him. He suddenly had eyes to see, ears to hear, and a mouth to speak, and he reached out to us during that time. On one occasion during those last three days in his hospital room, some of the family decided to get coffee from the café in the lobby. His unexpected comment was authoritative and powerful, something he had never exhibited before.

"No," he commanded. "The coffee shop doesn't open until such and such a time. You can go then, but now I want you to come here and talk to me."

My wife, Sham, commented to someone on the phone, "My father-in-law is more alive now on his deathbed than throughout his life!" It was the difference between *zoe* and *bios*.

That is what happens when a man who has been worshipping lifeless idols is suddenly made alive through Christ. He becomes like the One he is worshipping, and the *zoe* life of Christ begins to bubble up from deep inside him like a river of living water.

What, Then, Is Worship?

When we worship as we were created and redeemed to do, we become alive with the life of the One we worship. For that reason, it is important for us to get a clear understanding of exactly what worship entails, and it is here that I think many Christians get sidetracked.

If asked what comes to mind when they think of worship, many people immediately focus on weekend worship services, and more specifically on the music and songs. You hear this attitude in statements like, "The preaching was good, but the worship just didn't do it for me," or, "I really like this church because the worship is great." We've all heard these kinds of statements (or even made them ourselves). This mentality reduces worship to what happens at a weekend service—or even worse, to just that portion of the service when we sing.

Ironically, the use of the word *worship* in secular contexts reflects a more accurate understanding of what worship really is. Continuing with the sailboat analogy we used earlier in the book, suppose you heard someone say, "John just worships his sailboat." What that person means is that John is obsessed with sailing and how he can take his sailing to the next level. He might have already spent a great deal of money to purchase his sailboat, but he is saving up to add improvements. He reads all the magazines and books he can find on sailing and sailboats; he goes to all the shows; he hangs out with other sailors who are as into it as he is.

In the course of time, he might even grow discontented with his own twenty-foot craft as he looks at the full-featured, thirty-foot beauty one of his friends just bought. So he begins to plan and think about moving up to a bigger and better sailboat, dreaming about how much more he'll be able to do, and how he'll be able to rise to the next level of the sailboating hierarchy.

As the sailing season comes to an end and he reluctantly puts his boat into storage, he continues to "worship" sailing by taking classes, buying books, and even planning a vacation to warmer climates where he can do some more sailing. He waits through the long winter, anxiously anticipating the day when he can put his sailboat back into the water.

Now think about it: Through all this time, no one has ever heard John say, "I worship you, sailboat." When he is with his sailing friends, he never says, "Let's all just take a moment and praise our boats." But it is clear, just the same, that John worships his sailboat; he is absolutely obsessed with it, and he adjusts all other life priorities around this one pursuit. Everything in his life flows from how his life will be enriched because of his sailboat.

The True Essence of Worship

This is the true essence of worship, whether you are worshipping a sailboat, a car, a career, another person, or the God of all creation. When you make God your priority—your object of worship—your response to Him in a worship service is most emphatically not all there is to worship, regardless of how emotionally moving it might be. True worship is the conviction that only God can satisfy your deepest longings—a conviction so strong that it causes you to adjust your priorities to get as much of God as you can.

So when you take a Bible course at a local college or

attend a Bible study at your church during the week, this is worship, because your goal is to learn more about this God who has redeemed you. When you are prompted to give to your church, a ministry or an individual whose need comes across your path, this is worship, because you derive more joy from what your offering will accomplish for His cause than from anything you might have bought for yourself with that money. You are honoring the God you love.

When you pray, whether for your needs or the needs of others whom God has placed on your heart, that is worship, because all prayer says in effect, "God, unless you do it, nothing will happen."

Attentive listening is worship. Stephen Hawking, probably the most brilliant physicist alive today, has an unbelievably crippling disease and can hardly move. But because of a desire to keep tapping into his brilliant mind, clever engineers have fixed him up with a device through which he can painfully and slowly type out words that are then synthesized into speech.

Can you imagine the patience it must take to listen to a speech delivered in that manner? Yet when he lectured at Cambridge University, the place was packed—standing room only. Why? Because he is so highly esteemed for his intellect that they didn't want to miss a single word. When you eagerly, attentively listen to God's Word as it is being taught or preached, that is an act of worship—not because the individual bringing the message is engaging, exciting, or charismatic, but because his subject matter (God and His Word) is worthy of your best attention.

When you put time into building and strengthening

your marriage, that is an act of worship, because you are making a declaration that you believe, as God's Word tells us, that marriage—a man and a woman coming together for a lifetime relationship—is a powerful symbol of the relationship of Jesus to His church, and you want your own marriage to reflect the love Christ has for His bride. Quality parenting is an act of worship, as you train up your sons and daughters to be God-fearing, worshipping individuals who promote the kingdom of God.

All sharing is worship. When our sailing addict shares his boat stories, some may be boring and rooted in pride, but most are a spillover of his joy of sailing. The man loves his boat, he loves what he feels when he sails and he wants others to know that joy and maybe persuade them to experience that joy for themselves.

So too when you give a book to a friend or invite her to church because Christ means so much to you and you want her to share in that joy, that is worship. Evangelism, therefore, becomes worship. Now we can make sense of Paul's exhortation, "Whether you eat or drink or whatever you do, do it all for the glory of God" (1 Corinthians 10:31). All of life is worship.

A Rehearsal for Eternity

So, you might wonder, if all of life is to be an act of worship to God, why do we even need to have worship services on the weekends—or any other time? The simple answer is that while our faith is personal, it is never private. While we might have some contact with fellow believers throughout the week, for the most part we are out there living in the world, loving and worshipping God largely as individuals. Weekend worship reinforces the fact that when we were regenerated by the Holy Spirit, we were also baptized into a worshipping community, one that we are commanded not to forsake (see 1 Corinthians 12:13; Hebrews 10:25).

If you study the book of Revelation closely, it is filled with pictures of worship, and in every instance it is corporate—individuals together falling prostrate before the throne, casting their crowns before the Lamb and declaring His majesty. Thus, corporate worship services can rightly be conceived of as rehearsals for eternity.

Surrendering to His Initiative

Second, in weekend worship you surrender initiative. William Temple gave one of the most succinct definitions of worship I have ever come across. He writes, "For to worship is to quicken the conscience by the holiness of God, to feed the mind with the truth of God, to purge the imagination by the beauty of God, to open the heart to the love of God, to devote the will to the purpose of God."[1]

In every case, He initiates and we respond. Weekend corporate worship is one setting in which you almost completely surrender initiative. Unless you happen to be the preacher, you have no control over the content of the sermon; unless you happen to be a worship leader, you have no input in the song selections. You have no control over who, if anyone, will be sharing a testimony—all of which means you are perfectly poised to respond to divine initiative.

Making It Count

With God ready and willing with His initiative, I

believe we have a real opportunity during the corporate worship experience to be truly transformed by His presence. But in order for that to happen, there are a few practical steps we must take.

The first step is very simple: We must make it a priority to be present during corporate worship, to make regular attendance a commitment rather than an option. When you settle this issue once and for all and commit to joining at least weekly with other believers in your local assembly, you are, in essence, declaring: "Lord, meeting with You and Your people is a priority for me, and I am going to do whatever I can to be there, to be ready to worship and be responsive to Your initiative so I can be involved in what You are doing."

Such a commitment might seem a bit radical in today's Christian culture where erratic attendance has become customary, but that attitude—that commitment to be present and accounted for—is, in and of itself, an expression of worship—before one song is sung or anything else occurs in the service.

While you're at it, coming on time is another practical sacrifice of worship, an active declaration that says, "God, I realize that I have had a busy week, and I realize it takes time for me to be prepared for Your presence. I know that all those things that happen in the worship service, before the pastor even brings his message, are not preliminaries but are part and parcel of the means by which You draw me from the outer courts into Your holy presence. Lord, You are so important to me that I want to be well prepared, and I will make being on time and ready to worship the very first offering I bring to You during the weekend services."

It really is as simple as that. Your on-time presence in the worship service positions you to receive all that God has taken the initiative to bring through the corporate setting.

But in addition to being present, you must also be fully prepared to respond to what God is doing. That means being rested and ready and putting away distractions that would dull your spirit to His initiative. So if the night before you find yourself playing video games or watching television until early in the morning, you are probably not going to be at your best on Sunday morning, prepared for worship.

God's presence—His initiative in your life—is worth the priority of being present, on time and putting aside the distractions that can so easily sidetrack you and keep you from experiencing His best.

A Word About Music and Singing

This is another part of the service where deliberate engagement is crucial if we are to worship—another opportunity for a response to divine initiative. Some of the songs we sing are prayers, so use them to address God. It might be the first time all day or all week that you have had a chance to pray. And if you have trouble finding the right words when you pray, that problem too is solved. The words are already there for you, written by gifted and passionate people hungry for God. Other songs are grand affirmations of God's majesty and power. They fill me with great hope, as when we sing songs such as "Lion of Judah" by Robin Mark.[2] Others will challenge and move us in the area of consecration, as when we declare together the words of "No Higher

Calling" by Greg Gulley and Lenny LeBlanc.[3]

What I am emphasizing here is the importance of personally and deliberately engaging in what is happening in the service, and during the music portion of the worship service, that means making a determined choice to worship with your heart, mind and lips, so that you become a part of the chorus of worshippers exalting God.

Prayer, Giving and the Word

As with our singing, so it is with our prayers; the prayer of invocation at the beginning of the service is an act of worship because through it we are saying to God, "If you don't 'show up,' if You will not bless us with Your Spirit's presence, this whole exercise is a waste of time—the preaching, the singing, everything. We might as well be doing something else."

In the prayer of invocation, we follow the psalmist's lead and plead, "Arise, O LORD, and come to your resting place, / you and the ark of your might" (Psalm 132:8). Of course, if you don't make it on time, you miss the whole prayer of invocation. So too with the pastoral prayer. Pay attention, enter in, make the pastor's prayer your prayer—a prayer for the local body of Christ.

Why is it worship to do so? Every time someone treats my wife well, I feel honored. So too with Christ: In praying for the church body, you are praying for Jesus' bride. You honor Jesus—and that's worship!

Similarly, when it comes to the offering, the giving of our resources is a time of worship, not a mere business transaction. Train yourself to think along these lines as the offering plate approaches and as you put your offering into it: *God, as I give You this money, I acknowledge that whatever else I could have gotten with it—a boat, a gourmet dinner, new clothes—none of those things will give me as much pleasure as what You will do with this gift in extending Your kingdom.* If you aren't there yet, if you can't say that with integrity (and God wants authenticity in our worship), then simply acknowledge that too as you give.

Finally, when others speak, either in preaching or in testimony, choose to be an active, engaged participant through listening, hearing and responding—because that, as you now know, is worship as well. Paying attention to someone's testimony is worship because it is a declaration of the good work of God in that person's life. As for the sermon, your attention tells God that His words carry weight with you because they are His—again, that's worship.

In a nutshell, then, there are five things we must know when it comes to the foundational spiritual discipline known as worship: 1) We have been redeemed to worship; 2) it does not cater to His ego but enlarges our souls; 3) we become like the object of our worship—alive in His life; 4) all of life is worship; and 5) corporate worship is simultaneously a rehearsal for eternity and a surrender of initiative to God.

Questions for Group Study

1. Reread the opening story of Henry Ward Beecher's brother. Have you ever been guilty of "getting worship wrong" by focusing on the preacher or the worship leader? What are some other ways we can "get worship wrong"?

2. Read Isaiah 44:13–20, and discuss the statement, "We become like whatever we worship." How did those described in the Isaiah passage become like the idols they worship?

3. Is it possible to worship someone or something other than God (in other words, to have an idol in one's life) without really knowing it? How can we avoid the "idol trap"?

4. If the essence of worship is to make God one's all-encompassing priority, how does that work out in one's daily life? What changes have been made in your life as a result of making God a priority? What changes still need to be made?

5. Why is corporate worship important? What can you do to enhance corporate worship for yourself and for others?

6. Take some time to pray together, asking God to show you how you can learn to worship Him—individually and corporately—in spirit and in truth (John 4:24).

Chapter 3

Scripture: Listening to His Voice

In his 2006 work *Eat This Book: A Conversation in the Art of Spiritual Reading,* Bible scholar and pastor Eugene H. Peterson writes,

> There is an enormous interest these days in the soul. In the church this interest in the soul is evidenced in a revival of attention in matters of spiritual theology, spiritual leadership, spiritual direction, and spiritual formation. But there is not a corresponding revival of interest in our Holy Scriptures. . . . It is a matter of urgency that interest in our souls be matched by an interest in our Scriptures—and for the same reason: They, Scripture and souls, are the primary fields of operation of the Holy Spirit. An interest in souls divorced from an interest in Scripture leaves us without a text that shapes these souls.[1]

This is a very appropriate warning for the journey we

are on—learning how to be transformed into His image through the power of the Holy Spirit. The Holy Scriptures are indispensable when it comes to catching the wind of the Spirit. And just like Psalm 115 formed the foundation text for our understanding of worship in the previous chapter, Psalm 19 serves the identical purpose for this chapter.

More Than Information

The psalmist refers to "the law of the Lord," which for our purposes is synonymous with the Word of God or Scripture. It begins with these words:

> The heavens declare the glory of God;
>> the skies proclaim the work of his hands.
> Day after day they pour forth speech;
>> night after night they display knowledge.
> There is no speech or language
>> where their voice is not heard.
> Their voice goes out into all the earth,
>> their words to the ends of the world.
>> (Psalm 19:1–4)

Two questions immediately arise. Why does a psalm celebrating the law of the Lord begin with creation's witness to its Creator? And why is that witness described as speech? (Notice the multiplication of "speech" words: *declare, proclaim, pour out speech, voice.*)

In our society today, we by and large think of words almost exclusively in terms of the information they convey. When we read the newspaper or watch the news on TV, we do so for the information they contain. In our workday world, the practically endless stream of words and messages that come at us through e-mails, Web sites, and cell phones subject us to a barrage of facts, figures, statistics—more information. Our conversations with neighbors, coworkers, strangers on the street, and even family members, are all largely communicating information—some of it needed, some of it repetitious and mundane, but unending, nonetheless.

Not surprisingly, we have learned to equate all words with mere information, and we tend to filter out whatever seems repetitious or irrelevant in a desperate attempt to avoid information overload. Unfortunately, without being aware of it, we have applied this same filter to Scripture as well. We think of the Word of God as just more words—words that contain and convey a large body of information about God.

The consequences of this mind-set are truly catastrophic. Once we have read the words of Scripture, once we know the stories, then any subsequent reading is inevitably boring. How many times can we read about David and Goliath, Daniel in the lions' den, Joseph's coat of many colors, Jesus walking on the water—and yes, even the story of His crucifixion and resurrection—and maintain any degree of interest, let alone excitement? So if we read the Bible at all, it rapidly degenerates into a mechanical exercise that has long since ceased to become a transformational agent in our lives.

A Transforming Dialogue

But what if we approached Scripture in a different way? In the opening words of Psalm 19, the author paves the way for a radical change in our understanding of God's Word. Let's go right back to Genesis 1, the first chapter of the Bible. God is speaking, not to a person, but into a shapeless conglomerate of matter and space (see Genesis 1:2). And as He speaks, something happens. He declares, "Let there be light" (1:3), and light is created. Yet again He speaks, creating the land and the seas we call earth. Over the course of six days, all of creation comes into being at the spoken word of God, culminating in the creation of Adam and Eve, the first humans.

Taken as a whole, Genesis 1 portrays God's spoken words shaping the shapeless and filling the emptiness. In the opening words of Psalm 19, David picks up that theme and represents God's creation as a megaphone proclaiming the glory of the One who brought it into being by His spoken word. Centuries later the Apostle Paul would confirm that God's creation gives clear testimony to His "eternal power and divine nature" (Romans 1:20).

Throughout the Old Testament, we find Him raising up a prophetic voice through individuals commissioned to declare His purposes. But let's be clear: When we read that the "word of the Lord came" to this prophet or that individual, we must get past the sense that God was merely co-opting someone for the purpose of getting out some important information to His people. Nothing could be further from the truth!

The experience of the prophet Jeremiah shows us the intensity with which God's word came to those He commissioned. The message that God had for Judah was a call to repentance and a warning of judgment to come, and it was clearly not something the majority of the inhabitants of Judah wished to hear. Jeremiah's obedience in delivering this strong word from God resulted in him being constantly insulted and reproached. But when he considered the option of keeping silent, he found that God's word was "in my heart like a fire, a fire shut up in my bones" (Jeremiah 20:9).

Or consider Hosea, who was a humble shepherd in Tekoa minding his own business when the word of the Lord came to him. Hosea was no mere mouthpiece for God's dictation but someone whose very life became a prophetic declaration of God's purposes to the nation of Israel. Even his name, which means "salvation," served as a prophetic message to God's rebellious people that if they would but turn to Him and repent, they would be saved. Through God's command for him to marry a woman who was a harlot, Hosea himself became a prophetic representation of God's love toward the impure and sinful Israel. After his wife bore three sons—whom God commanded Hosea to name "God Scatters," "No Mercy," and "Not My People" as prophetic representations of how God would deal with unfaithful Israel—she abandoned him and returned to a life of harlotry. In yet another prophetic picture, God commanded the prophet to find his wayward bride, bring her back home and continue to love her, just as God pursued and loved unfaithful Israel. Far from merely delivering information dictated to him from above, Hosea embodied the message—his entire domestic life became a living, breathing prophetic representation of the word of God.

As we continue reading further in the prophets, we find them engaging in a dialogue with their audience—God's people. We encounter false prophets arguing with the true prophets of God. The final book of the Old Testament, Malachi, actually becomes an extended dialogue between God's prophet and God's wayward people, with a skeptical majority hardening their hearts to God's call for repentance while a small minority turns their hearts and are saved.

When we consider this sweeping portrayal of God's word in the Old Testament, it is evident that "the word of the Lord" is not primarily words that communicate information but a creative event, a fire in a man's bones, a commandeering of a man's whole domestic life, divine speech that demands a response, a relational interaction that either hardens or softens the listener.

A Voice Calling in the Desert

Malachi is followed by the blank pages between the Old and the New Testaments in our Bible, representing four hundred years of prophetic silence. And then suddenly, without warning, we read in Luke 3:2 that "the word of God came to John . . . in the desert." What were among the first words out of his mouth? "A voice of one calling in the desert" (3:4). Four hundred years of prophetic silence did not change the equation of "the word of the Lord" to a voice that addressed people.

John's task was to pave the way for Jesus who, according to John's Gospel, is called "the Word" (John 1:1). I don't know a single other individual named "Word." Why then was Jesus called "the Word" or Logos? It drives home the stunning truth that the same Word that created the heavens and the earth and then shaped and filled them, the Word that was a fire in Jeremiah's bones, the Word that took over Hosea's domestic life, the Word that through Malachi engaged the people of God in a transforming dialogue, the Word that possessed John and drove him out of the wilderness bursting with a message he could not contain, that Word was now incarnate in a human voice that would speak audibly.

As we read through the Gospels, it becomes clear that everything that the Word of the Lord did when it came through the voice of men in the Old Testament, Jesus' words did in the flesh. He created bread and fish. His Word called people. Tax collectors and fisherman dropped whatever they were doing and began following Him. To them, the Word of Jesus wasn't information but an invasion of their lives.

Jesus' Response to Scripture

Because Jesus is the Word incarnate, how He responded and related to Scripture is of vital importance to us. Does it bear out our understanding of the Word of God as a voice that speaks and draws people into a dialogue, a relationship with the speaker? There are two passages—one in the Old Testament and one in the New Testament—that are crucial to our understanding of how Jesus approached Scripture.

Isaiah 50:4–5, one of the key "Servant of the Lord" passages in Isaiah and one that Bible scholars identify as messianic, gives us a glimpse into the mind of Christ and offers a clear answer as the Messiah speaks prophetically: "The Sovereign LORD has given me an instructed tongue, to know the word that sustains the weary. He wakens me morning by morning, wakens my ear to listen like one being taught. The Sovereign LORD has opened my ears, and I have not been rebellious; I have not drawn back."

According to this Scripture, Messiah's tongue has

been instructed by listening to His Father's voice. And how did the Father speak to Him? That is answered in the relevant New Testament passage—Hebrews 10:5–7:

> Therefore, when Christ came into the world, he said:
> "Sacrifice and offering you did not desire,
>> *but a body you prepared for me;*
> with burnt offerings and sin offerings
>> you were not pleased.
> Then I said, 'Here I am—it is written
>> about me in the scroll—
>> I have come to do your will, O God.'"

This passage in Hebrews includes a quotation from Psalm 40; I have put the words "but a body you prepared for me" in italics because the corresponding line in Psalm 40 is translated "my ears you have [opened.]"

Here's the mental picture that these verses conjure up. I see Jesus coming to His Father with the open scroll—the Word of God—in hand, saying, "You are not interested in 'sacrifice and offerings.' You are not interested in 'doing devotions' or other religious rituals. But Father, I believe there is a personal word about Me written in this scroll and You have opened My ears to that word. I want You to speak to Me, so that I may have Your law firmly embedded in My heart."

When you put Isaiah 50, Psalm 40 and Hebrews 10 together, it is evident that Jesus responded to the Word of God, not as mere information, but as the voice of His heavenly Father speaking personally to Him so that He might have appropriate words to sustain the weary listeners that thronged to hear Him speak. What the Old Testament unfolded, what John the Baptist exemplified, Jesus confirmed by His approach to Scripture.

Such a perspective on Jesus' relationship to the Word of God also helps us understand a recurring phrase found throughout the Gospels. We read that something Jesus said or did happened "so that the Scriptures might be fulfilled." Some skeptics, even Bible scholars, read this and immediately conclude that Jesus, deluded as He was with Messianic pretensions, deliberately set out to fulfill Scripture.

The huge problem with this view is that many of the Messianic prophecies—such as the manner of Jesus' death—were beyond the powers of a pretender to orchestrate. Rather, the Gospels portray a Jesus increasingly conscious that His entire life was scripted. It turns out that He is the central actor in a five-act play. (I am indebted to N.T. Wright for this framework.)

Act One is *Creation*—where Psalm 19 begins. Act Two is *The Fall*, when our first human ancestors rebelled against God and plunged all of creation into chaos. Act Three is *The Calling of Israel*, through whose pure worship of Yahweh and glad obedience to His law God would put the world right. But Israel by her rebellion became part of the problem.

That set the stage for Act Four: *Jesus*, who got His cues from Acts One, Two and Three. As Jesus listened to His Father, the divine dramatist interpreted for Him the meaning of Acts One, Two and Three and how He should respond. Hence the verse from Hebrews that we have already looked at—"It is written about Me in the scroll; My ears You have dug out for Me. I have come to do Your will."

See how it all hangs together? The Word of God is the voice of the Lord that calls us into a relational encounter with the speaker, changing us. Jesus, Himself named the Logos (Word), related to the Scriptures in exactly the same way and lived a life scripted by that same Word of God.

But what about Act 5? That's where we come in. Just like Jesus, as people who are in the process of being conformed to His image, we too are intended to play *our part in this great drama* of redemption. Like Jeremiah, Hosea and Malachi, like John, Jesus and Matthew, we too are intended to listen to His voice in and through the Scriptures that we might live divinely scripted lives.

How vastly different, how gloriously different than words that merely communicate information! It is this understanding of the Scriptures that radically changed my *emotional* approach to the Scriptures. I would be bankrupt if someone took them away from me. I would lose my bearings on how to live if I didn't have the prophetic script.

Delighting in His Word

The author of Psalm 19 certainly felt this way.

The law of the LORD is perfect,
> reviving the soul.
The statutes of the LORD are trustworthy,
> making wise the simple.
The precepts of the LORD are right,
> giving joy to the heart.
The commands of the LORD are radiant,
> giving light to the eyes.
The fear of the LORD is pure,
> enduring forever.

The ordinances of the LORD are sure
> and altogether righteous.
They are more precious than gold,
> than much pure gold;
they are sweeter than honey,
> than honey from the comb.
By them is your servant warned;
> in keeping them there is great reward. (19:7–11)

"The law of the LORD is perfect, *reviving the soul*" (19:7). We encounter the identical phrase in Psalm 23, when David likens himself to a needy sheep and pictures God as a shepherd who leads him to lie down in pastures of succulent green grass, and who "restores my soul" (23:3).

In his delightful and moving book *A Shepherd Looks at Psalm 23,* Phillip Keller recounts his own days as a shepherd when he would be pressed to find and restore a sheep from his own flock that had gone astray. Noting that a "cast" sheep, one that has fallen and turned over on its back, will quickly die if not soon righted, Keller writes that he would set out with a sense of urgency to find a "cast" sheep, and "more often than not I would see it at a distance, down on its back, lying helpless." Keller would swiftly run to the forlorn creature, set it on its feet and, "straddling the sheep with my legs I would hold her erect, rubbing her limbs to restore the circulation to her legs" all the while whispering in its ear to comfort and restore it to a calm and rested state.[2]

What a beautiful picture of how God uses His Word to restore us, coming to us in our downcast and hopeless state, energizing us and whispering words of comfort and restoration! Because His Word is comprehensive ("perfect"), there is no situation or circumstance that He cannot speak into in this way.

The "statutes of the LORD are trustworthy, making wise the simple" (19:7). In wisdom literature, of which the Psalms are a large part, a "simple" person is one easily deceived, naive (perhaps even morally so) and hence led astray. But God's Word will drive out that simplicity and replace it with wisdom.

Aren't you glad that you don't have to be a scholar, that you don't have to know Greek and Hebrew for this to happen? Don't get me wrong—I am very thankful to God for Christian scholars who have mastered the intricacies of Greek and Hebrew, and I am tremendously indebted to them. My point is, you and I don't have to be put off by the fact that we are not experts in order to become wise. Every day brings with it all kinds of perplexing situations, from parenting a difficult child to handling a relative who is not following God. The law of the Lord is able to make us wise and sure-footed in such circumstances.

"The precepts of the LORD are right, giving joy to the heart" (19:8). You see, sometimes obeying God's Word is neither pleasurable or desirable, but we do it because it is right. And along with that obedience comes a unique, undefinable sense of wholeness at the very center of our being. That is called integrity, and that will lead to a joy that far exceeds the temporary joy of disobedience.

Have you ever felt like lashing out at someone—giving him a piece of your mind for the way he treated you? It feels good in the heat of the moment; if it didn't, you wouldn't be tempted to lash out. But later you discover this nagging sense of guilt and "dis-ease" that is hard to shake. Biting our tongues (self-control), refusing to give in to the temptation and instead speaking the "soft answer [that] turns away wrath," (Proverbs 15:1 NKJV) denies us the immediate, short-lived pleasure that lashing out gives, but then we can luxuriate in the far more abiding pleasure that comes from knowing "I did what was right."

"The commands of the LORD are radiant, giving light to the eyes" (Psalm 19:8). This speaks of illumination—somewhat akin to the statutes of the Lord making simple people wise, but it includes another dimension. When we see the commandments as radiant, we see them as beautiful. Usually before we go to sleep at night, Sham will read the newspaper. Every now and then she will exclaim, "Honey, look at this," and then read a section from one of the advice columns. After hearing the answers spouted by the self-appointed experts, my thoughts run along these lines: *Lord, when I put Your Word alongside such drivel and nonsense, how brilliantly it shines!* That's when I know the commandments are radiant.

I trust you are getting the picture. The psalmist seems to ransack language to find six different adjectives for the Word of God and six different phrases to describe what it accomplishes in six different dimensions of our being—our soul, our naïveté, our heart, our eyes, etc. Is it any wonder that he finds the law of the Lord to be "sweeter than honey" (19:10)? Where does he get such delight in the Word of God?

It comes from seeing the Scriptures not as a collection of words that give us information but as the voice of the living Lord; He has indeed dug out our ears and written a personal word concerning me in His book.

Delight flows first out of a conviction that the divine dramatist keeps coming alongside us, prompting us to play our part and then actually hearing, responding and experiencing what the psalmist experienced in Psalm 19. So let's get down to the practical principles of hearing His voice in His Word.

Learning Our Lines

1. *Read the Bible—all of it—and read it regularly.* I am not an actor, but people who are tell me that at the first rehearsal, the first thing the cast members do is read the whole script. Why? Because they all know that each person is more likely to act his or her part better when he or she understands the big picture. On the occasion of my father's eightieth birthday and my parents' fiftieth anniversary, my seven-year-old niece performed a fifteen-minute recitation from *Aladdin*, flawlessly playing all the parts in that section. She knew the whole play by heart and therefore had no trouble adjusting her voice and accent for each character she played.

What if we knew the Bible like that, so that we could effortlessly move from incarnating ourselves as Jeremiah at one moment and Isaiah at another? We could be the tax collector, standing before God and saying, "Lord be merciful to me," and then Moses standing before the burning bush, taking off our shoes. We might actually begin to *live* the script. It is this that Eugene Peterson captures in a single brilliant sentence: "It takes the whole Bible to read any part of the Bible."[3]

I have also found it helpful when repeatedly reading the Scriptures to think of the process as *learning a new language.* Have you ever wondered how babies eventually learn to recognize their names or when they are being addressed? They can't do this a day or two after birth. It takes five or six months before they turn their heads when their name is called. How many words has the child heard by that time? Millions, probably. It takes immersion in a language we don't understand for it to become a voice that personally speaks to us.

Reading the Bible repeatedly from cover to cover does that for us. For many years I have made it a practice to read through the entire Bible once every year, and I can't begin to tell you how I have grown from this discipline. If that kind of regimen seems too overwhelming for you, then break it down into smaller pieces. There are various Bible-reading plans that take you through the whole Bible at various speeds. As you read, don't worry about the parts you don't understand. Remember, you are not, at this stage, reading to analyze or understand. You are immersing yourself in a new language. One day you will hear.

2. *Meditate on select portions.* The psalmist ends the psalm with these words: "May the words of my mouth and the meditation of my heart be pleasing in your sight, O Lord, my Rock and my Redeemer" (19:14). It is evident that Psalm 19 was not a hastily composed "ditty" but the result of prolonged meditation on its grand subject: the law of the Lord.

What exactly is meditation? A quick foray into Bible reference works reveals six different root Hebrew words that are translated "meditate" twenty-two times in the Old Testament. The combined meaning of these six words gives us this definition of meditation: *giving serious consideration and careful, undistracted thought to a subject; it may include speaking the thoughts out loud to oneself in low tones, or reviewing the material to establish or clarify proper thought in order to respond properly to the information.*

If you prefer pictures to word definitions, however exhaustive, think of a dog with a favorite bone. He gnaws it till it's bare, drops it, kicks it around, picks it up again, all the while growling with evident pleasure. That's what the psalmist did with the law, resulting in his delightful poem.

One oft-recommended way to meditate is to read a short passage of Scripture—out loud, slowly—several times throughout the day and week. That's the "speaking to oneself in low tones" part of our definition. Another way, one that John Piper has recommended, is to pick out one or two verses that lodge in your heart during your reading, write them down on a note card and review them several times throughout the day. Repeat the process each day. Still another way, one Bill Hybels calls "saturation meditation," involves taking one passage and reviewing it several times a day, every day, for a whole year. I know of one person in my congregation who did this with Psalm 139, and it made a significant impact on her life.

3. *Pray the script.* Personally, I find the most effective way to meditate is to turn the passages I read into prayer. Psalm 19 implies this. It begins with "The heavens declare the glory of God; the skies proclaim the work of his hands" and ends with "May the words of my mouth and the meditation of my heart be pleasing in your sight, O Lord." He shifts from speaking to us about God's Word to addressing God.

Out of the twenty-two references in Scripture to

meditation, nineteen are found in the Psalms—Israel's prayer book. Remember also what we have already learned—that Scripture is the voice of the Lord pulling us into a life-changing dialogue with Him. And we take our cues from His words to us. When someone speaks to us, we speak back in ways that naturally correspond to what he or she says to us. If asked, "How was your vacation?" we are not likely to respond with, "Are those new shoes you're wearing tonight?" So too with God's Word. His Word to me (when I read it) provokes and shapes a corresponding response. Here's how Psalm 19 might shape a parent's prayer for a son away at school:

> Father, today use Your Word to enliven my son wherever he may be feeling a loss of energy and zest for living. Make him wise through Your law, so he sees through any lies he may encounter in his lectures. When tempted to do wrong, may he choose to obey Your commandments, trusting that he will find more joy in doing so than in the temporary pleasure of sin. May the insights from Your Word help him think clearly in moments of perplexity. May Your law also reveal to him Your infinite holiness so he may also experience the fear of the Lord that is the beginning of wisdom. As he reads Your Word today, may it not be boring or mere duty, but may he experience delight in it. May it convict him of any sin and lead him to wholehearted confession that his conscience may remain sensitive. May his whole life be pleasing to You.

Obedience

Read the script, meditate on select portions, pray the script back to God and finally, *act the script.* That's the whole point of the script, isn't it? Notice how the psalmist, after celebrating this magnificent law, also affirms that "by them is your servant warned; in keeping them there is great reward" (19:11). Obedience is critical—especially when, you recall, our overarching purpose is transformation into His likeness.

Remember how God fed the children of Israel as they wandered in the desert for forty years? Manna miraculously appeared each morning. God commanded them to gather just enough for their needs each day and no more except the day before the Sabbath when they could gather twice as much. Of course, there were some who thought they could improve on God's plan and took more than they needed for that day. They tried storing the excess, but when they got up the next day to eat it, they found it had rotted and become a breeding ground for maggots.

Perhaps this can serve as an analogy of what happens when we receive God's Word but refuse to do anything with it. In his book *Take and Read,* Eugene H. Peterson quotes Julian Green, who noted:

> The story of the manna gathered and set aside by the Hebrews is deeply significant. It so happened that the manna rotted when it was kept. And perhaps that means that all spiritual reading which is not consumed—by prayer and by works—ends by causing a sort of rotting inside us. You die with a head full of fine sayings and a perfectly empty heart.[4]

A friend in Phoenix, a gifted writer, once taught on meditation in an exercise class she attends and teaches. At the end of the class a lady came to her and shared a pithy summary of transformation through Scripture: "I eats myself full [I read the script], I thinks myself clear

[I meditate on the script], I prays myself hot [I pray the script] and I lets myself go [I obey the script]." Couldn't have said it better myself!

Questions for Group Study

1. The author contends that many people today read the Bible with the intent of gathering "mere information," but God intends us to have a "transforming dialogue" with the Scriptures. What is the difference? Discuss this issue in the light of Isaiah 55:10–11 and Hebrews 4:12.

2. The author says that, as people who are being conformed to Christ's image, we are to live a life "scripted" by the Word of God. What does it mean, in practical terms, to take this approach to Scripture?

3. Reread Psalm 19:7–11, and share examples from your own life of how God's Word has revived your soul, shown you wisdom, given you joy, enlightened you, etc.

4. Which of the three principles for hearing God's voice in His Word (reading, meditating and praying) do you practice most regularly? Which of these do you need to develop?

5. Discuss some practical ways we can act on and obey God's Word and so be conformed to the image of Christ.

Chapter 4

Study:
Renewing the Mind

In their landmark 1992 book, *No God but God: Breaking With the Idols of Our Age,* editors Os Guinness and John Seel offer the following deeply troubling analysis of the church today:

> Contemporary evangelicals are no longer people of truth. Only rarely are they serious about theology. Both problems are a tragedy beyond belief. . . . Vaporized by critical theories, obscured by clouds of euphemism and jargon, outpaced by rumor and hype, overlooked for style and image and eroded by advertising, truth is anything but on the march . . . modern sources of authority such as politics, psychology and management theory routinely eclipse Biblical authority in practice. The combined effect is to render unthinkable the notion of an evangelical community that is defined by truth, united by truth and guided by truth.[1]

And David F. Wells echoes the refrain:

We have the makings of a kind of faith whose life is only tenuously related to the Word of God, that is not much nurtured by it, that is not anchored in the character and greatness of God and that is almost completely unaware of the culture that surrounds it.[2]

Ouch! That hurts. And for a radical rather than a superficial healing of that hurt, we need to understand and commit to the spiritual discipline of study—yet another sail to catch the wind of the Spirit. And as with the disciplines of worship and Scripture, my goal in one brief chapter on a vast subject is to create a hunger for something based on an understanding of its importance.

An Objection—and a Response

Perhaps you find yourself reacting negatively to the very word *study*. "That may be all right for the intellectual types, those who know Greek and Hebrew, and like to read deeply," you might say. "I'll read the Bible, and maybe get into a good Bible study from time to time. But disciplined study—that's not for me."

I won't ignore the fact that some individuals are more inclined toward intensive study than others. God created each of us with different aptitudes, and not everyone is inclined to intensive study—not even Scripture study. But let's recall that Jesus said we are to love God with all our heart, soul, mind and strength (see Mark 12:30), and He did not emphasize one over another. Usually we think of loving God as something we do with our heart—our will and emotions. We may also talk about loving God with our strength—our actions and physical effort. But how often do we consider our mind—the rational part of our being—as an appropriate avenue to express our love for God?

Jesus' first followers were hardly a group of educated intellectuals. They were largely fishermen and tax collectors from little towns and fishing villages in first-century Palestine. And yet, Jesus encouraged them to love God with their minds. Years later, the Apostle Paul writes to the believers at Corinth, reminding them of the intellectually humble background from which most of them came:

> Brothers, think of what you were when you were called. Not many of you were wise by human standards; not many were influential; not many were of noble birth. But God chose the foolish things of the world to shame the wise; God chose the weak things of the world to shame the strong. (1 Corinthians 1:26–27)

Elsewhere in this same letter, Paul explains that as Christians, we have "the Spirit who is from God, that we may understand what God has freely given us" (2:12). Noting that the person who does not have the Spirit of God cannot receive the things of God (see 2:14), he goes on to identify the one element that every believer possesses, that qualifies each and every one of us—regardless of our intellectual aptitude or our educational background—to be students of the deep things hidden in God's Word: "We have the mind of Christ" (2:16).

Convincing ordinary believers that they have what it takes to study God's Word was so important that the Holy Spirit directed Paul to say it again, this time in his letter to the Ephesians. Paul writes in:

> Then we will no longer be infants, tossed back and

forth by the waves, and blown here and there by every
wind of teaching and by the cunning and craftiness of
men in their deceitful scheming. Instead, speaking the
truth in love, we will in all things grow up into him
who is the Head, that is, Christ. (Ephesians 4:14–15)

Notice again the emphasis: All Christians, not just a
few gifted ones, are intended to move beyond infancy
to the point where they would not be easily swayed by
wrong teaching.

Not convinced yet? Consider then Hebrews 5:12: "In
fact, though by this time you ought to be teachers, you
need someone to teach you the elementary truths of
God's word all over again." The writer here isn't addressing a select group of individuals. He didn't administer
a gifts survey to these saints, set aside just those individuals who demonstrated an aptitude for teaching and
scold them, "You guys should be teachers by now." No,
he is writing to an entire community years after they
had become Christians, and he is communicating his
concern that after all this time they should be mature
in the faith, spiritual meat eaters rather than still exist-
ing on the milk of the basic fundamentals of the faith.
While they should have such an understanding of the
truths in God's Word that they can teach them to others,
in reality they are still largely unacquainted "with the
teaching about righteousness" (5:13).

If you put the words of Christ together with the
teachings of the apostles and throw in the counsel of
many of the writers of the Old Testament, it becomes
clear that growing into a mature spiritual thinker is part
of the calling of all believers to become progressively
shaped into the image of Christ.

A Unique Adventure for Each of Us

One final observation before we launch into the specifics. Let us not forget that engaging the mind through study is more than just mental gymnastics or a mere academic discipline. Studying God's Word is part of the larger commandment God has given us to love Him with our minds. We must see the discipline of study firmly in the context of a relationship with Him because we are to love God with all of our minds. We are not to approach the study of Scripture in some objective, detached manner like we might study rocket propulsion or quantum physics. We study with a goal in mind, and that goal is to grow progressively in our love and devotion to God.

Because God desires a relationship with us, and because we are all unique individuals, this loving God with our minds plays out in different ways for different people. God has a way of appealing to us so that, if we are attentive to His Spirit, we will respond to this call to love Him with our minds. Take, for instance, my good friend Miles, a dynamic pastor and a passionate preacher, well schooled in God's Word. There could not be two more different individuals than Miles and me. When I got the call to be a Christ-follower, I was in my first year of engineering. I knew how to study and had a natural inclination toward intellectual pursuits. By contrast, when Miles got the call to be a Christ-follower, he was a drug addict who could hardly speak a complete sentence.

Within a few months of my becoming a Christian, I was devouring Scripture along with a wide range of books on the Christian faith. After Miles came to Christ, he would sometimes come into my office, sit down and say, "Sunder, I'm not going to do anything else except read the Bible and listen to your sermons." But there came a day when God began to work on Miles, and he came to me one day and said, "Sunder, I want to go to Bible college and become a preacher."

"You know, Miles," I said, "you are going to have to expand your horizons and begin reading other books now, and find out what God is showing other men and women of God." And that is exactly what he did. He read different authors, engaged with his professors, researched and wrote papers for his classes, passed his exams, and today he is an engaging preacher and pastor who speaks annually to our congregation. Miles and I are completely different individuals with different backgrounds and different temperaments, and yet each of us has been called to love God with our minds.

And so it is with you as well. "This study business is not for me" is no excuse. Knowing God, studying His Word and loving Him with our minds are for every single one of us. The ways we each express our obedience in this area will be unique to how God created us and to the background He's given us. All of us, however, will find ourselves loving our study of God because we love the God whom we are studying. This is what we were created and saved for. Consider what happened to our minds at our salvation.

The Redemption of the Mind

The correct starting point is the Apostle Paul's description of the natural mind (before you became a Christ-follower) in Ephesians 4:17–18: "So I tell you this, and insist on it in the Lord, that you must no longer live as the Gentiles do, in the futility of their thinking. They are darkened in their understanding and separated from the life of God because of the ignorance that is in them due to the hardening of their hearts."

Paul's description of our natural mind—ignorant, darkened and futile—is not, you understand, a commentary on the intellectual ability of those who do not know Christ. The world is filled with brilliant men and women who neither know nor care anything about Christ; they may accomplish great things, solve knotty problems and change our world, but Scripture declares that without Christ, their thoughts are futile. They are "darkened in their understanding and separated from the life of God" (Ephesians 4:18).

This tells us that there is a dimension of divinely inspired critical thinking—divine wisdom—that is missing from the minds of those who don't know Christ, and the consequence of this missing link is a worldly, natural wisdom that ultimately leads to futility. The Greek word for "futile" in the New Testament carries the same meaning as the word "vanity" in the book of Ecclesiastes. When the thoughts and achievements of a mind that does not have the light of Christ do result in something of ultimate good, it is because of what theologians call "common grace"—God's grace operating on unregenerate minds.

But as Paul explains, in regeneration through Christ, we "have taken off [our] old self with its practices and have put on the new self, which is being renewed in knowledge in the image of its Creator" (Colossians 3:9–10). The very thing that was missing in our natural state—that which rendered our thinking futile—is now within us.

This doesn't mean our minds immediately become new when we turn to Christ, but they gain the capacity to be renewed progressively in knowledge—to be remade in the image of our Creator. God takes a mind that was darkened in its understanding, ignorant and futile in its thinking, and turns it into a mind that is free to be renewed in righteousness, in knowledge and in the image of Christ.

If regeneration by the Spirit makes our minds renewable, who is responsible to actually do the renewing? Scripture is clear: It is our job! Paul tells us that as believers we are no longer to be conformed to this world's wicked pattern of thinking and acting, "but be transformed by the renewing of your mind" (Romans 12:2). Yes, God takes our darkened, futile, ignorant minds and transforms them, making them capable of being renewed in knowledge, righteousness and the image of God. But it is our responsibility—indeed, it is our privilege—to take our renewable minds and make them progressively newer. But this is no easy matter because we have a powerful adversary who is battling for our minds.

Our Enemy

That is why we find Paul expressing his fear to the Corinthians that "just as Eve was deceived by the serpent's cunning, your minds may somehow be led astray from your sincere and pure devotion to Christ" (2 Corinthians 11:3). Notice that Paul doesn't say he is concerned about their hearts being led astray, but their minds. This is not an issue of our emotions, but of our minds. We can love God fully with our emotions and yet have our thinking thrown off track if we are not plugged in to the discipline of study. Think back to how Satan tricked Eve. Did he appeal to her emotions? No, he used logic and smooth reasoning.

Likewise, your mind is a major battlefield in the realm of spiritual warfare, and there is a cunning and well-equipped enemy who is trying to lead you astray by appealing to your mind. Paul is referring to this realm when he writes:

> The weapons we fight with are not the weapons of the world. On the contrary, they have divine power to demolish strongholds. We demolish arguments and every pretension that sets itself up against the knowledge of God, and we take captive every thought to make it obedient to Christ." (2 Corinthians 10:4–5)

Paul makes this warfare sound like an intense conflict with imposing weapons that are demolishing heavily reinforced strongholds, and so it is. However, it is not a flesh-and-blood battle but one that takes place largely in the realm of the mind. Have you ever thought of your mind as a potentially furious battlefield? It is there that the enemy comes against you with arguments and rationalizations that set themselves up against the knowledge of God. And you must be diligent in taking every opposing thought captive and obedient to Christ—discerning such twisted thinking and replacing it with the corresponding truth in Scripture.

In summary, then:

- First, our unredeemed minds are darkened and our thinking is futile;

- Second, when we are regenerated by the Holy Spirit, that same mind becomes capable of being renewed in knowledge and righteousness;
- Third, the progressive renewing of that renewable mind is our responsibility;
- Fourth, this is not an easy task because we have a cunning and crafty enemy who works hard to lead our minds astray with arguments and rationalizations that oppose what God has revealed in His Word about His nature, being and works;
- Fifth, we have to take these thoughts captive and make them obedient to Christ.

To say that the discipline of study is "not for me" is to surrender to the enemy one of the most strategically important arenas of your Christian life.

Arguments and Rationalizations

Our enemy is not a wooden-headed, one-dimensional foe with a "one size fits all" strategy for all believers. We are unique, and he deals with us according to our unique weaknesses and foibles. You can be certain that he knows just the right buttons to push to get our thoughts moving in the wrong direction. Remember, his goal is to keep us from renewing our minds through meaningful, consistent study, and he has many ways to do that. Here are a few of his favorites:

a) *Insufficient time.* We often tell ourselves we don't have the time to study God's Word. What is the divine truth that we need to set in opposition to this lie? Paul writes, "Be very careful, then, how you live—not as unwise but as wise, making the most of every opportunity, because the days are evil. Therefore do not be foolish, but understand what the Lord's will is" (Ephesians 5:15–17).

Paul is exhorting us to use our time wisely—"making the most of every opportunity." Another translation (NJKV) uses the phrase "redeeming the time." When slaves were brought to the market, a buyer would "redeem" them by paying the selling price. Paul uses "redeem" elsewhere to describe our deliverance from the slavery of sin. The concept Paul is getting at here might be framed in this way: "Your time has become enslaved by the enemy, and you need to redeem it, buy it back, whatever the cost." Why? The phrase "make the most of every opportunity" is an attempt to capture the sense of one of the Greek words for time: *kairos*, referring not to the *quantity* of time (so many hours or minutes) but to its *quality*. We need to get serious about managing the *quantity* of time (the word *chronos* in Greek), so we do not end up missing the *quality* (*kairos*) moments—in other words, striking when the iron is hot—because the days are evil and we need to understand what the will of the Lord is.

Just as we don't all have an equal amount of financial wealth at our disposal, we are not all equally "wealthy" in the time we have for study. Some of that has to do with the season of life in which we find ourselves. For example, if you have a newborn baby who wakes up five times every night and two toddlers to look after during the day, time is definitely limited.

Here's how one young couple in a similar situation put Paul's exhortation to buy up the time into action. They were taking part in a special evening Bible study at our church and felt so prompted by the Holy Spirit to diligently complete all the homework for the study. But, of course, that meant fitting this into an already tight schedule. So how did they do it? They explained, "We just set our alarm to go off a couple of hours earlier, and we spent that time working on the Bible study assignments." That's one way to "make the most of every opportunity." Obviously the specific solution—getting up two hours earlier—is not the point; the mind-set behind the solution is.

b) *Amusements.* Interestingly enough, the root word in "amusement" comes from the Latin *muse*, which means "to think." But do you know what happens when you put the letter "a" in front of *muse*? You get the word *amuse*, which literally means "not thinking." Amusement is unthinking activity.

What comes immediately to mind is television. Several years ago I read a very powerful book by advertising executive Jerry Mander, entitled *Four Arguments for the Elimination of Television.* This insightful analysis of the havoc wreaked by TV was a real eye-opener for me. (Now, don't get me wrong: I am not a crusader against TV. I will watch news and sports programs from time to time, but I am mindful of the subtle way in which it can insinuate itself into our lives and never let go.)

During the years he spent preparing his book, Mander kept an informal record of the terms people use in ordinary conversation to describe how they felt about television. In all he recorded about two thousand conversational and written descriptions. He described the concrete details of what goes on between viewer and television set to three psychologists, famous partly for their work with hypnosis. One of them said to him, "It sounds like you are giving a course outline in hypnotic trance induction." She added that "since television images move more quickly than a viewer can react, one has to chase after them with the mind. This leaves no way of breaking the contact and therefore no way to comment on the information as it passes in."[3]

What a double whammy TV delivers! It steals time from study that can renew our minds and at the same time, it influences our thoughts with almost no critical thinking to counter it. "But I find it so relaxing before I go to bed," you might say. "It helps me unwind after a busy day." Mander debunks that too with unarguable research. TV does the very opposite—it agitates us. Chalk that up to yet another hugely successful rationalization of the enemy.

c) *Laziness.* In his best-selling book *The Road Less Traveled,* author M. Scott Peck asks this riveting question which each of us would do well to consider: "Since the path of spiritual growth, albeit difficult, is open to all, why do so few choose to travel it?"[4] In the context of our present conversation, we might pose the question this way: Why do so few choose to hoist the sails to catch the wind of the Spirit?

The answer Peck offers will most likely hit close to home for you as it has for me: "It is our laziness . . . that causes us . . . to stay at the comfortable, easy rung where we now are or even to descend to less and less demanding forms of existence."[5] He relates a story about a client he had treated years before that powerfully illustrates the point. The client, a woman caught in a web of dysfunctional relationships that were controlling her life, came to Dr. Peck for help in extricating herself from the mess she was in.

Through careful coaching and mentoring from Dr. Peck, she began drawing proper boundaries, confronting some of the individuals and finding some freedom. Peck recalled that this woman came to his office one day bubbling over with joy as she shared with him the progress she had made in one particular relationship. He listened to her for a time, sharing in the victory she was experiencing and then pointed out to her that she could have this kind of freedom in all the other relationships in her life.

Her response to his simple suggestion could not have been more shocking to Peck. She exploded in anger, saying, "But that would require me to be thinking all the time! . . . I didn't come here for my life to be made more difficult. I want to be able to just relax and enjoy myself." Shortly afterward she canceled her counseling sessions, too afraid to deal with her problems.[6]

The truth of the matter was that this poor lady didn't want to face the prospect of thinking for the rest of her life. Nothing "amusing" about that. Her reaction reminded me of a one-liner from humorist Don Marquis: "If you make people think they're thinking, they'll love you; but if you really make them think, they'll hate you."

Undoubtedly, our clever and cunning enemy has many more rationalizations and arguments up his proverbial sleeve in this battle for our minds, but the three I have drawn to your attention will give you some insight into his ways.

The Stakes Are High

And in case this isn't enough to stimulate us to love God with our mind, perhaps it will help to look at the cost of not renewing our minds, of not engaging in this battle for our intellect:

a. *Doubt.* We become vulnerable to doubt (something else the enemy can use for his advantage) and rendered insecure. In *God in the Dark: The Assurance of Faith Beyond a Shadow of Doubt,* Os Guinness writes:

> To think and not understand is one problem; not to think and have no chance of understanding is a greater one. A keen mind will rarely remain idle and satisfied. If the faith by which it lives does not allow it room to move, the mind is apt to exact its own revenge. A good mind denied by bad faith will self-destruct with insecurity, guilt, fanaticism, or doubt.[7]

As believers we have the mind of Christ, and that means we can face with confidence the questions and issues that challenge our faith on a day-to-day basis. The Christian walk is not easy, as Christ Himself tells us (see Matthew 7:13–14). There are many difficult situations that will challenge to the very core what we believe and what God's Word declares. We are not to shrink back or be afraid of facing the challenges that come our way. Like the Bereans, we must dig into God's Word to find out what we believe and why we believe it (see Acts 17:11). That means reading what other men and women of God have to say, studying the issues that confront us and engaging in dialogue with other believers—and with unbelievers.

A word of caution here: Remember the relational dimension of your intellectual pursuits. So read, think, talk, examine, argue, etc. But don't forget to bring God into the dialogue too. It is the key to a robust faith that will endure. One of the most important principles I have picked up as a pastor counseling individuals who are facing challenges to their faith is this: When you are struggling with doubt, never suspend obedience to the things that are clear because of the things that are unclear. Too often people find themselves shipwrecked in their faith when dealing with specific issues of legitimate doubt, and they end up suspending their faith and obedience altogether. The key to victory is to continue in the things that you are confident about in your faith while you are exploring the things that you are not clear about.

b) *Legalism and mediocrity.* This consequence of not thinking also happens to be, ironically, one way of dealing with some doubts. Gordon MacDonald addresses this in his book *Ordering Your Private World*:

> Some Christians appear to be afraid to think. They mistake the gathering of facts, doctrinal systems, and lists of rules for thinking. They are uneasy when dealing with open-ended questions. And they do not see the significance of wrestling with great ideas if they cannot always come up with easily packaged answers. The consequences are a drift towards mediocrity in personal living and mental activity and a loss of much that God meant for His children to enjoy as they walk through creation discovering His handiwork. Life under such circumstances becomes amusement, function without thought.[8]

c) *Capitulation under stress.* Flabby minds render us unfit for the endurance that suffering demands. A positive example illustrates what I mean. Some readers will recall back in 1979 when more than fifty Americans were taken hostage in the U.S. Embassy in Iran and held there for more than 440 days. Among them was Kathryn Koob, who became a tremendous example to the other hostages for the way in which she blessed those around her during the entire crisis. The other hostages all agreed that Kathryn was a real source of inspiration and inner strength to them during the entire crisis. When asked afterward what enabled her to respond like this, she attributed it to years of reading and committing to memory what she read. In her mind was an incredible storehouse of truth that she could draw upon to sustain herself and inspire others in a time of difficulty.[9] We may never be held hostage or face the rigors of imprisonment, but the truth holds. Those who love God with their minds, who engage in the spiritual discipline of study, will likewise have a reservoir of insights to draw upon to sustain themselves and others in times of suffering, whether extreme or modest.

Next Steps

Study Guides. I prepare a study guide for most sermons I preach during weekend worship services at our church. That way those who have listened to me have a chance to dig a little bit deeper during the week. (This is a good reason to take notes during the sermon if you don't have access to a similar resource.) As I noted earlier in this chapter, Acts 17:11 is a wonderful biblical mandate for reviewing during the week what you hear on Sunday: "Now the Bereans were of more noble character than the Thessalonians, for they received the message with great eagerness and examined the Scriptures every day to see if what Paul said was true."

We know that Paul was an apostle anointed by the

Holy Spirit, but who were these Bereans? They were ordinary Christ-followers, and yet they were daring to say, in effect, "We are going dig into the Scriptures to check out for ourselves what we just heard Paul preach." Now Scripture doesn't chide these Bereans for an anti-institutional suspicion of Paul, or for not having a teachable spirit; instead, it commends them.

You should do the same—check whatever you hear from your pastor or other Bible teachers against Scripture. By all means receive the messages eagerly, but examine the Scriptures during the week. Use all available study guides and your own notes to dig into the subject. Naturally, if you find anything indicating that your pastor or a teacher didn't handle a passage accurately, then he needs to know, for his benefit and yours. I have often reiterated this to my own congregation, inviting them to challenge me in love if I speak something that cannot be backed up by the Word of God.

Small Group Study. I believe that community study is absolutely critical to loving God with our minds. Paul writes: "Let the word of Christ dwell in you richly as you teach and admonish one another with all wisdom, and as you sing psalms, hymns and spiritual songs with gratitude in your hearts to God" (Colossians 3:16). Here is an anointed apostle encouraging laypeople to teach and admonish one another. You gain additional insight when you study a topic with a group of individuals who are eager to know God.

Several years ago, I had the privilege to sit in on a group study of the book of Mark during a ministry trip in Turkey. I heard many keen insights into this Gospel account. The study leader turned to me and asked, "Sunder, what are you picking up from this discussion?" I had been listening carefully and identified two or three recurring strands from what different people were saying. As I summarized them, it suddenly occurred to me that all of them were pertinent to the situations these international workers in Turkey were facing at that moment.

This demonstrates the value of study in groups as a dynamic means of discerning God's voice in the here and now. If you ever leave your worship service not quite sure of what God might be telling you in the sermon, it might become clear at your midweek small group study, if you are part of a Berean-minded group. If not, join one.

Audio Teaching. In the previous chapter, we discussed the importance of understanding Scripture as the drama of redemption, as the divine script in which we learn to hear God's voice. But we all know that some parts of Scripture are hard to understand, and we must know how to approach these difficult areas. Several years ago I preached one whole sermon on each book of the Old Testament. I didn't quite make it through all thirty-nine books, but I covered all the historical books and five of the prophetic books. Then two years ago we did "Highway 27," which included one sermon on every book of the New Testament. So in all we have covered about fifty-two of the sixty-six books in the Bible, one sermon for each book.

I suggested to our congregation that they might take the tapes of these sermons and, starting with Genesis, devote one week for each book in the Bible. By the end of that year, I suspect their grasp of the divine drama of redemption would be a lot clearer than when they started. You might have access to similar material from your church or via the Internet. The variations on study through audio sermons are many; what is needed is determination to start and persevere.

Books and Reading. There is no shortage of good Christian books on just about every imaginable topic. Many of us have been readers our whole lives and have no problem picking up titles on subjects we feel God has placed on our hearts to study. But the sheer number of books, good books, is intimidating for those seeking to begin this discipline of study. "Where do I start? What should I read?" might well be your bewildered response.

If so, I might be able to help. One project I have decided to complete before my time on earth is over is to compile a list of fifty books that have most impacted my life, books I would like to leave as a spiritual legacy for my children and grandchildren to pursue. So far, I have a list of thirty-seven books by fifteen different authors that you will find at the end of this chapter. Thirteen of these are in italics and represent a good starting point.

Here's another tip: If you find an author who has particularly impacted you, find out what other books that author has written. Not every book by a writer will be equally powerful, of course, but there is a good chance that you will be deeply blessed by most if not all the works of certain authors. Some who have served this function for me include Gordon MacDonald, C.S. Lewis, John Piper, Eugene Peterson, and N.T. Wright.

Finally, whether you are a beginner or a seasoned reader, your focus should be on depth and retention, not on the number of books you read. Jesus' parable of the sower declares that the good soil, that which produced a harvest, stood for a noble heart that *retained* the word and by persevering brought forth fruit (see Mark 4:1–20). How do you increase the retention factor?

We all know that most books have a few blank pages at the back. When I read a book, I use those pages to write notes on anything that strikes me in the book, such as a quotation or passage, something I might want to reference in the future, a "hot idea" for personal growth or ministry worth further reflection and implementation, etc. When I also take the time to write a brief summary of the chapter, reviewing the thrust of the book is a "piece of cake."

Certain chapters of some books are so crucial that I write a one- or two-paragraph summary of that chapter. I have done that with several books that have impacted me. It might take a little extra time to write out a summary, but if your goal is retention, it's worth the effort. And it becomes a relatively simple matter to review the book at a later date.

A Step Beyond

Beyond these resources are seminars and workshops on such topics as marriage or discipleship, sponsored by your church or a parachurch organization. You might even consider taking courses at a college or seminary.

However you pursue the spiritual discipline of study, as you dive in, you will find yourself embracing the truth of the Apostle Paul's exhortation to the Philippians: "Finally, brothers, whatever is true, whatever is noble, whatever is right, whatever is pure, whatever is lovely, whatever is admirable—if anything is excellent or praiseworthy—think about such things" (4:8).

Recommended Reading List
(Italicized titles are good to start with.)

Os Guinness
> *The Call*
> No God but God

John Piper
> *Desiring God*
> Future Grace
> Don't Waste Your Life
> Let the Nations Be Glad
> The Supremacy of God in Preaching

Gordon MacDonald
> *Ordering Your Private World*
> Rebuilding Your Broken World
> Rediscovering Yourself
> The Effective Father

R.C. Sproul
> *The Holiness of God*

Eugene Peterson
> A Long Obedience in the Same Direction
> Leap over a Wall
> Answering God
> Reversed Thunder
> Under the Unpredictable Plant
> *The Jesus Way*

Elizabeth Elliott
> Through Gates of Splendor
> *Shadow of the Almighty*

C.S. Lewis
  Mere Christianity
  The Problem of Pain
  The Great Divorce
  Miracles
  Letters to Malcolm

Ben Patterson
  Waiting
  Serving God

Peter Kreeft
  Making Sense out of Suffering

Dallas Willard
  Hearing God
  The Spirit of the Disciplines
  The Divine Conspiracy

Mark Buchanan
  Your God Is Too Safe
  Things Unseen
  The Rest of God

Erwin McManus
  Seizing the Divine Moment

Peter Scazzero
  Emotionally Healthy Spirituality

John White
  Daring to Draw Near

Ron Sider
  Rich Christians in an Age of Hunger

Questions for Group Study

1. Reread the quote from Os Guinness and John Seel at the beginning of the chapter. Is this a fair assessment of the evangelical church today? Why or why not?

2. The author says that some people react negatively to the word *study*. What is your reaction? Does the author's description of study as a "unique adventure" appeal to you? Why or why not?

3. Read Acts 17 and compare the people of Thessalonica, the people of Berea, and the people of Athens. What attitudes in these three groups affected their ability to receive truth?

4. Review the three rationalizations and the three costs (or consequences) for not taking up the discipline of study. Are there others?

5. Read Romans 12:2. What are some of the methods the author mentions for renewing the mind? What ones are you currently practicing? What ones are you thinking of beginning?

6. Identify one book on the list at the end of the chapter (preferably one that is italicized) that you would like to read this year, and resolve to do it.

Chapter 5

Prayer

Many years ago during my first ministry sabbatical, I had the privilege of taking a course on prayer from one of my favorite authors and theologians, Dr. Eugene Peterson. By that time, I had already read all of his books I could get my hands on, and I was thrilled to have the opportunity to study with him in person. This was long before the days of PowerPoint presentations, and so as Dr. Peterson stood before the group, he took a plastic transparency, placed it on an old overhead projector and wrote out two simple words with a well-used green felt-tip pen: "Jesus Prays."

Then he looked up and declared that these two words—"Jesus Prays"—represent the very foundation for any and all Christian prayer. That's a good starting point for our consideration of the fourth discipline that helps us be conformed to the image of our Savior.

In Luke 11:1 we read, "One day Jesus was praying in

a certain place. When he finished, one of his disciples said to him, 'Lord, teach us to pray, just as John taught his disciples.'" Prayer permeated Jesus' life and ministry. In Mark 1:35 we read, "Very early in the morning, while it was still dark, Jesus got up, left the house and went off to a solitary place, where he prayed." In Luke 6 we are told that before He took the history-changing step of choosing twelve apostles from among His first disciples, Jesus "went out to a mountainside to pray, and spent the night praying to God" (6:12). In John 17 we're privileged to listen in as Jesus intercedes to the Father for Himself, His disciples and all those who would one day believe upon His name. Finally, in the Garden of Gethsemane, where He chose to keep moving toward the cross and drain the cup of God's wrath against human sin, the burden of prayer became so intense that "his sweat was like drops of blood falling to the ground" (Luke 22:44).

Prayer characterized His life and ministry—not only on earth, but also after His resurrection and ascension. Scripture tells us that He continues to pray for us: "Therefore he is able to save completely those who come to God through him, because he always lives to intercede for them" (Hebrews 7:25).

Here's the staggering implication: If Jesus, fully God and man, loved by the Father with infinite love and full of the Holy Spirit without measure, saturated His whole life in prayer and has continued to pray for us for more than two thousand years, we have absolute assurance that *prayer is never a wasted effort.* Whenever we pray, we are sharing in a divine activity, something that we cannot affirm with equal certainty about anything else we might choose to do. Must we not, therefore, join with the disciples in their request of the Master, "Lord, teach us to pray"?

This is not only true of personal prayer but equally so when it comes to corporate prayer. When Jesus entered the temple and drove out all the money changers and the people selling and buying sacrificial animals, He declared, "It is written, . . . 'My house will be called a house of prayer'" (Matthew 21:13). Notice that He didn't call God's house a "house of teaching," even though Jesus taught a lot in the temple. Nor did He call it a "house of healing," though Jesus definitely healed in the temple. He also didn't call it a "house of fellowship," although the temple was a major gathering place for God's people. He called it one thing: a "house of prayer for all nations" (Mark 11:17).

Likewise, our churches are to be centers of prayer. For that reason, in the church I pastor, we have tried to make prayer foundational to every activity and pursuit. That is why we shut down all other ministries in our church for the first full week of every year and meet every night of that week for prayer, especially prayers of repentance. Then once every month throughout the year, we hold "concerts of prayer," seeking for the Spirit's anointing on all our ministries. Also, every September we devote each Sunday night to pray for an unreached people group that we as a congregation have adopted. Our elders meet four times a year on a Saturday morning to spend several hours together in prayer. A good portion of every staff meeting is devoted to prayer, and various groups meet at various times during the week to pray for needs close to home and far away. This commitment to prayer, however modest, is all because Jesus said, "My house shall be called a house of prayer."

More Than Mere Words

Jesus gladly responded to His disciples' request for training in this crucial spiritual discipline, and in the prayer He taught them, we find a pattern we can follow. But before He taught them how to pray, He first addressed how *not* to pray: "And when you pray, do not keep on babbling like pagans, for they think they will be heard because of their many words" (Matthew 6:7).

The English Standard Version of this verse renders the phrase "do not keep on babbling" as "do not heap up empty phrases," and the context here is important. The Gentiles in Jesus' day believed that the more words they used in prayer, the more they were likely to be heard by God. Consequently, their prayers were often characterized by continual repetition of certain words and phrases. And they were empty (or vain) presumably because they could be chanted with the mind totally disengaged. So Jesus said, "Don't pray like that; follow this pattern," and recited what has become known as "The Lord's Prayer":

> Our Father which art in heaven, Hallowed be thy name. Thy kingdom come, Thy will be done in earth, as it is in heaven. Give us this day our daily bread. And forgive us our debts, as we forgive our debtors. And lead us not into temptation, but deliver us from evil: For thine is the kingdom, and the power, and the glory, for ever. Amen. (Matthew 6:9–13, KJV)

Because this prayer is so easy to memorize, our praying it might begin in earnest but easily degenerate into the very mindless repetition that Jesus warned against.

So it is important to remember that Jesus taught His disciples this prayer to drive home to them, and us, that our praying needs to be intentional, systematic and substantive. Of course, this isn't to imply that prayer cannot be spontaneous or passionate. God wants our communion with Him to be characterized by passion and emotion as we pour out our hearts before Him.

Our Father in heaven, hallowed be your name.

The word *hallowed* comes from a root that means "set apart, unique." And His name is His character. So in the opening movement of this prayer, we are to express our desire that God be recognized for who He is—that there is none other like Him in nature and being, infinitely holy and glorious. This was clearly Jesus' dominant agenda in His own prayers to the Father:

> Father, the time has come. Glorify your Son, that your Son may glorify you. . . . I have brought you glory on earth by completing the work you gave me to do. And now, Father, glorify me in your presence with the glory I had with you before the world began. (John 17:1, 4–5)

Toward the end of this prayer, in which He prays with compassion for His people, Jesus says, "Father, I want those you have given me to be with me where I am, and to see my glory, the glory you have given me because you loved me before the creation of the world" (17:24). Even Jesus' prayer for His people is bracketed by a preoccupation with the glory of God. Jesus is teaching us to pray like He prayed—asking Him to bring about a universal recognition of His glory.

Thy kingdom come, Thy will be done on earth as it is in heaven.

At first sight, it might seem that these phrases represent two separate requests; in fact they are one and the same. To pray "Your kingdom come" is the same as praying "Your will be done on earth" because the kingdom of a king is under the rule of that king, and the rule of that king represents his will.

The gospel chronology suggests that after Jesus prayed His glory-saturated prayer in John 17, what followed was His agonizing prayer in Gethsemane, which was all about God's will being accomplished on earth. "Father, if you are willing, take this cup from me." Nevertheless, He continued, "not my will, but yours be done" (Luke 22:42). Once again Jesus is teaching us to pray like He prayed. So in *our* prayer we ask that glad-hearted obedience to God's will, flowing out of a passion for His glory, will increasingly characterize life on earth right now.

Of course, even as He prayed in Gethsemane, Jesus already knew the will of His Father—go to Jerusalem, be condemned as a false Messiah and be crucified for the sins of the world. In His case, prayer was a crucial part of the process by which Jesus aligned His will with the already known will of the Father. So it is for us. Because the bulk of God's will is revealed to us in Scripture, to pray like Jesus prayed, we need to pause long enough to ponder what God's will is in the requests we bring before Him. What cues has He given in His Word that allow us to pray for ourselves—and for others—in such a way that we follow the divine script? Let's look at one example of this in Scripture.

Pondering—and Praying—God's Will

In the book of Acts, we find that as the disciples first began to proclaim Jesus' name to the world, they faced enormous obstacles. Called before the Sanhedrin, they were threatened with severe punishment and ordered to cease and desist immediately. How did they respond to such persecution? They joined together in strategic, thoughtful prayer—not a mechanical, wooden repetition of the prayer that Jesus taught them, but certainly using that as their model:

> When they heard this, they raised their voices together in prayer to God. "Sovereign Lord," they said, "you made the heaven and the earth and the sea, and everything in them. You spoke by the Holy Spirit through the mouth of your servant, our father David:
> > 'Why do the nations rage
> > and the peoples plot in vain?
> > The kings of the earth take their stand
> > and the rulers gather together
> > against the Lord
> > and against his Anointed One.'
>
> Indeed Herod and Pontius Pilate met together with the Gentiles and the people of Israel in this city to conspire against your holy servant Jesus, whom you anointed. They did what your power and will had decided beforehand should happen. Now, Lord, consider their threats and enable your servants to speak your word with great boldness. Stretch out your hand to heal and perform miraculous signs and wonders through the name of your holy servant Jesus." (Acts 4:24–30)

As you read this, do you detect the theme of God being glorified, of His name being hallowed? It permeates the entire prayer. The opening phrase, "Sovereign

Lord," followed by a recounting of how God created the heavens and earth, is not a mindless repetition of "Hallowed be your name," but gives the name specific content—Sovereign Creator. The prayer also ends with a request that too is an overt and heartfelt expression of the desire for God to stretch out His hand to perform glorious miracles. The whole prayer is bracketed by a preoccupation with God's glory.

How about God's will? Are they praying that the will of God be done? The disciples quote from Psalm 2, because in that psalm they recognize striking similarities between David's situation and theirs, making it eminently suitable to guide their specific requests. The disciples knew God's Word, and they used it to appeal to Him in their situation. The concluding request, "Now, Lord, consider their threats and enable your servants to speak your word with great boldness" (Acts 4:29), reflects David's closing words in Psalm 2, in which he preaches boldly to king and rulers. They know that they have to do the same, and they ask for the power to obey.

Focusing God's Will

To capture the essence of this kind of creative yet artful application of the Lord's Prayer, I framed this definition: *Prayer is focusing the will of God, as revealed in the Word of God, on a situation that is out of line with His Word, to bring it into harmony with His will.*

Earlier in this book, we analyzed the story of Peter's first meeting with Christ and were able to isolate four elements that are essential to conversion:

1. *Divine initiative,* and God usually takes that initiative through His Word;

2. *A realization of who Jesus really is; that Jesus is the sovereign Lord of creation,* not just a good teacher or a godly example;

3. *A realization of our core identity before Christ as sinners,* who can't stand in God's presence and are in need of His mercy;

4. *A response of faith that follows Jesus to progressively realize our new identity* as His people.

Now let's take these four elements and think about how we could apply them in prayer for someone to come to Christ. Of course, we could just pray fervently, "Lord, bring John to Christ, make him a Christian," and we would all agree that this is praying according to God's will, since Scripture tells us that God is "not willing that any should perish, but that all should come to repentance" (2 Peter 3:9, KJV). But what if we took this account of Peter's introduction to Christ, and used those elements in our prayer for John?

"Father," we might say, "please exercise your awesome power to overcome John's passivity and lack of interest in the gospel and *send* someone [divine initiative] who will proclaim Your Word to him boldly and accurately." I have heard many testimonies of people in which someone preached the Word of God to them, and later it was revealed that someone else had been interceding for them.

Next we might pray, "Lord, show John that You are more than just a great teacher or an admired religious leader. Show him that You are the sovereign Lord of the universe. And while You are at it, Father, show him who he is at his very core—a sinner in need of your mercy —and the salvation that Jesus has provided freely for him. Humble him by Your holiness. May he know that he is a sinner who cannot stand in Your presence. Grant him the gift of repentance and awaken in him a faith that will prompt him to forsake all and follow You. Help John make a clean break with his past."

So whether it is an apostolic prayer for boldness in witness or the conversion of a loved one, they are both guided by "Thy will [revealed in Thy Word] be done in earth, as it is in heaven." It is hard to imagine a greater contrast to the vague, timid requests that we all too often come to Christ with, asking God to bless so-and-so, or to be with this or that group "in a very real way." What do those prayers even mean? They come dangerously close to the babbling of Gentile prayers that Jesus warned against.

Praying Beyond Our Needs

After establishing the foundation of prayer upon God's glory and His will, Jesus teaches us to pray for specific needs, beginning with our sustenance: "Give us today our daily bread" (Matthew 6:11). Remember, Jesus is providing us with a prayer pattern here. He does not mean that all we should ask God for is our daily food. God is our provider for all things in every circumstance, and so "our daily bread" is everything from the food we eat to the clothes we wear, the house we live in—every conceivable need we have.

It also includes the whole area of employment and career—the work God has given us to do to earn a living. Most people have to work for their "daily bread," so praying for a job or for your business to prosper comes within the context of asking God for your daily bread.

Next we are to pray, "Forgive us our debts, as we also have forgiven our debtors. And lead us not into temptation, but deliver us from the evil one" (Matthew 6:12–13). Broken and strained relationships in our lives are matters to pray about, not ignore. We also need to pray that He will keep us from any kind of trials (another translation of temptation) that may cause our enemy, the devil, to triumph. This is an "advance" prayer for success in the specific temptations and life trials that threaten to trip us up.

These "need" petitions are often the only kind of prayer God ever hears from many believers. A majority of us never get beyond the "me, myself and I" mentality of intercession. But by placing these needs in the middle of His model prayer, Jesus is challenging us to go deeper, beyond our own needs.

While reflecting on this, I was reminded of a story I read about a fighter pilot who one day decided to put his jet plane into a steep ascent. He was disoriented, however, and was flying upside down, so when he pulled back on the stick to pull his plane up, in reality he was executing a steep power dive right into the earth, where he perished.

In a spiritual sense, focusing only on our own needs is upside-down intercession, which will ultimately keep us from soaring in prayer. By contrast, right-side-up praying begins, "Hallowed be your name," and "Your kingdom come, your will be done," followed by the petitions for our needs. Jesus is emphasizing that our petitions must be rooted in the larger context of the spread of God's kingdom for the universal recognition of His glory.

Examples of "Right-Side-Up" Prayer

How do you practically position your prayers so that God's glory stands firmly at the center? Let's say you are in need of a job and income, so you turn to the Lord in prayer. An upside-down prayer might go something like this: "Lord, I need a job, and You know that I am going for this interview tomorrow. Please help me in this interview, and allow me to land this job." If you have been unemployed for some time, your prayer might even include statements like, "Lord, don't You care how much I am suffering? Why are You doing this to me? Please just help me! I can't take much more!"

Of course, God is our Father (Jesus' prayer opens with this emphasis); He understands our needs and weaknesses and graciously hears even these kinds of prayers. But Jesus is teaching us to move beyond spontaneous and need-centered exclamations into prayer for personal needs set in the larger context of a desire for God's glory and God's kingdom. So we might pray this way:

> O Lord, You are sovereign over all my circumstances, including my ability to get a job. I know that You are well able to deal with the financial affairs of any particular company and You can create a job opening for me in whatever company that You want. I know that You are absolutely sovereign over timing as well. The decisions of other people are not going to control my employment because You care for me and will open the proper door. You are absolutely sovereign and You can and will do it at just the right time. I confess that You are good and that my present circumstances do not call into question Your goodness toward me. I pray that when I get this job, it will be done in such

a way that nobody else gets the glory that belongs to You, and I will be able to tell everybody that this is how my God provides for me. Father, because I still have to knock on doors and still have to write resumes, help me not to put my trust in one single human resource, even though human beings will be involved in the process. Let me put my trust in You, keeping in mind Your promise to give me my daily bread.

That is praying for a pressing personal need in context of God's glory, of "hallowed be your name." Now how about further prayer for the same need, this time in the light of "your kingdom come, your will be done"? We might continue our prayer in this way:

Father, Your Son declares in Matthew 6 that I am of greater value than the birds and the flowers, and so I am going to eagerly look forward to see the way in which You are going to provide for this need in my life. And when You do, I am going to tell people how faithful You have been to me. You also told me that I don't have to be anxious, so I ask You to so fill me with Your Holy Spirit that I can demonstrate to my family and friends that I am trusting You. Because You also told me to seek first Your kingdom and righteousness, please help me during this time of waiting and deprivation to identify with all of my suffering brothers and sisters all over the world who don't even know where their next meal will come from. Also, please make real to me Your admonition that I cannot live on bread alone, but by every word that comes from the mouth of God (see Deuteronomy 8:3, Luke 4:4), so that in these days when I don't know where my bread is going to come from, I can feed on Your Word. May that Word become more precious to me than ever before and allow me to lead my family in such a way that they too will be able to respond in faith in a sovereign God.

Can you see the difference between "upside-down" prayer where human need is prominent and "right-side-up" prayer shaped by His Word and dominated by a larger concern for God's glory and the spread of His kingdom?

Pulling It All Together

Here in the proverbial nutshell are the insights that our journey through Jesus' model prayer has yielded:

- Prayer is never a wasted effort. It's what Jesus is doing today.

- Prayer is an expression of our desire for God to be universally recognized as glorious, and therefore, we ask Him to bring that about.

- Prayer is focusing the will of God as revealed in the Word of God on a situation that is out of line with the Word of God, to bring it into harmony with His will.

- Prayer for our personal needs must be rooted in the larger context of the spread of God's kingdom for the universal recognition of His glory.

In the light of this, can you see how prayer is linked to worship, Scripture and study—the spiritual disciplines we dealt with in the previous chapters? We grasp His glory in worship and so we seek its spread in prayer; we grasp His will in the broad sweep of Scripture and shape and fill our prayers accordingly; as study helps us love God with our minds, our prayers are lifted beyond the stifling boredom of cliché-ridden babbling and become a source of delight to us and an inspiration to others.

Finally, just as in the discipline of study we can learn from our brothers and sisters both past and present, in the same way we can learn to pray "the Jesus way" through the prayers of others. Over the years one of the major resources I have used is a volume entitled *The Valley of Vision: A Collection of Puritan Prayers and Devotions*. Here is one prayer from this book. Read it slowly, reflect upon the mind and heart from which such a prayer poured forth, and then read it aloud as a prayer of your own to God:

> O Holy Spirit,
> Vain are all divine purposes of love
> and the redemption wrought by Jesus
> except thou work within,
> regenerating by thy power,
> giving me eyes to see Jesus,
> showing me the realities of the unseen world.
> Give me thyself without measure,
> as an unimpaired fountain,
> as inexhaustible riches.
> I bewail my coldness, poverty, emptiness,
> imperfect vision, languid service,
> prayerless prayers, praiseless praises.
> Suffer me not to grieve or resist thee.
> Come as power,
> to expel every rebel lust, to reign supreme and keep me
> thine;
> Come as teacher,
> leading me into all truth, filling me with all
> understanding;
> Come as love,
> that I may adore the Father, and love him as my all;

Come as joy,
to dwell in me, move in me, animate me;
Come as light,
illuminate the Scripture, moulding me in its laws;
Come as sanctifier,
body, soul and spirit wholly thine;
Come as helper,
with strength to bless and keep, directing my every
    step;
Come as beautifier,
bringing order out of confusion, loveliness out of
    chaos.
Magnify to me thy glory by being magnified in me,
and make me redolent [i.e., having or emitting a
    pleasant odor] of thy fragrance.[1]

A Transformed Community

And we rise from such prayers transformed, though
sometimes unaware. In the book of Exodus, we read
about how God's announcement of His decision to
destroy the children of Israel prompted Moses to intercede for the nation. Scripture tells us that as he prayed
for them on Mount Sinai, his communion with God was
so special and intimate that when he came back down
to the people, his face actually glowed with God's glory
(see Exodus 34:29–35). But it was a fading radiance. The
greater glory of the new covenant in Jesus is that prayer-
wrought transformation that does not fade but increases
steadily, in us and others.

> Therefore, since we have such a hope, we are very
> bold. We are not like Moses, who would put a veil
> over his face to keep the Israelites from gazing at
> it while the radiance was fading away. . . . Now the

Lord is the Spirit, and where the Spirit of the Lord is, there is freedom. And we, who with unveiled faces all reflect the Lord's glory, are being transformed into his likeness with ever-increasing glory, which comes from the Lord, who is the Spirit. (2 Corinthians 3:12–13, 17–18)

At its best, prayer is a preoccupation with God's glory. Through such prayer we become partakers of His glory and touch the lives of other people, so that His "ever-increasing glory" defines the entire body of Christ.

Questions for Group Study

1. Read Matthew 6:7. Jesus warns us not to allow our prayers to be "babbling" or "empty phrases." What does this mean? How can we avoid this error?

2. The author says that the Lord's Prayer (Matthew 6:9–13) is a pattern for how we should pray. Read it together and identify some of the attitudes that we should have in prayer and what kinds of things we should pray for.

3. The author defines prayer as "focusing God's will, as revealed in His Word, on a situation to bring it back into line with His Word and His will." How do your prayers fit this definition? How do they differ?

4. What further prayer principles can you glean from Abraham's prayer in Genesis 18:22–33 and Moses' prayer in Exodus 32:1–13?

5. What is the difference between "upside-down" prayer and "right-side-up" prayer? How does praying "right-side-up" help to transform us into Christ's image?

6. Reread the Puritan prayer at the end of the chapter, and identify concepts that you could rephrase into your own words and use as your own prayers.

Chapter 6

Confession: Pursuing Holiness

"Catching the wind of the Spirit" is a dynamic phrase that inspires thoughts about moving forward in our spiritual life, of gaining momentum in our journey toward Christlikeness. Hopefully that's been happening to you as we have together explored, over the last several chapters, a few of the vital spiritual disciplines by which we cooperate with the Holy Spirit in this journey. We have looked at *worship,* our response to God's initiative in all aspects of life. We have considered *Scripture* as the voice of the Lord, pulling us into a vital dialogue with Him. We have learned how we may love Him with our minds by embracing the discipline of *study.* And in the previous chapter we have explored what *prayer* as Jesus taught us might look like.

But what about those times that we all experience when we find ourselves losing momentum, even going backward in our journey toward Christlikeness? Instead of demonstrating the Spirit fruit of love, we behave selfishly; instead of living joyfully, we grumble and are unthankful; instead of being peacemakers and facilitating reconciliation, we find ourselves embroiled in conflict, even initiating it; instead of exhibiting patience, we explode in anger because we just can't wait.

Instead of worshipping the living God, we worship His creation; instead of listening to the voice of God in Scripture, we listen to the voices of people around us and embrace the wisdom of this world; instead of loving God with our minds, we waste time in unworthy pursuits, even filling our minds with thoughts that are hurtful, damaging and sinful. Instead of devoting ourselves to prayer, we forget God "days without number" (Jeremiah 2:32) and forge ahead with our plans, supremely confident of our own ability to succeed.

What is the answer? How do we go forward when we have been going backward? Thankfully, God has provided a way, and it is found in the very important spiritual discipline called confession.

A "Bad" Confession

While most of us may have an intellectual understanding of what confession means, we need to go beyond this because it is crucial not just *that* we confess, but that we confess *appropriately*, the kind of confession that God is looking for. Let's begin by taking a quick look at what confession is not. A few years ago, Elliot Spitzer, then the governor of New York, was exposed as having been in a long-term relationship with a prostitute. When the story came out, he was forced to face the media and the public at-large—to confess his sins, so to speak. I recall listening to his first public statement on the matter and was struck by the words he used to "confess" his wrongdoings. Here is what he said:

> Over the past nine years, eight years as attorney general and one as governor, I've tried to uphold a vision of progressive politics that would rebuild New York and create opportunity for all. We sought to bring real change to New York and that will continue. Today, I want to briefly address a private matter. I have acted in a way that violates my obligations to my family and that violates my—or any—sense of right and wrong. I apologize first, and most importantly, to my family. I apologize to the public, whom I promised better. I do not believe that politics in the long run is about individuals. It is about ideas, the public good and doing what is best for the State of New York. But I have disappointed and failed to live up to the standard I expected of myself. I must now dedicate some time to regain the trust of my family.[1]

In reflecting on what Mr. Spitzer said, we instinctively realize that something is not quite right. His statement seems a bit hollow and insincere (if you had the opportunity to watch it on video that tone of insincerity would have hit you even more dramatically). What is wrong with this "confession"? First of all, he focuses on image management, beginning by pointing out all the wonderful things he did during the previous nine years.

Next, there is a definite attempt to minimize his misdeeds with his high-toned declaration, "I do not believe that politics in the long run is about individuals," which really means, "What I do privately really doesn't affect all the public good that I have done." Perhaps most important, he doesn't specify what he did wrong but merely offers vague generalities about having violated "obligations to my family" as well as an undefined "sense of right and wrong."

In fact, though his visibly hurt and distraught wife is standing next to him, he doesn't even acknowledge her existence, or the violation of the vows of faithfulness he made to her. As I watched, I had the uneasy sense that the whole thing was nothing more than a scripted production aimed at political damage control.

Mr. Spitzer's "confession" really seemed to have more to do with regret at having been exposed than it did with true repentance, and for us it serves to contrast a mere façade of confessing with what is true, life-transforming biblical confession.

Radical Confession

Perhaps the most thoroughly articulated confession in the entire Bible is the one prayed by King David, a man whose sins of adultery and murder were far more serious violations of God's laws than those of which many of us will ever be guilty. Nonetheless, his confession and repentance serve as a true biblical model that each of us can follow. The Bible story begins with the observation that at a time when David should have been leading his army in battle, he was lounging on the palace roof. In other words, he was in the wrong place at the wrong time, a combination that usually leaves one an easy target for being drawn into sin.

As he was strolling around, he happened to see a

beautiful woman, and he was immediately smitten with a lustful desire for her. Because he was the king, David had all the pull he needed to get what he wanted, and what he wanted was this woman, Bathsheba, even though she was the wife of another man. As the story unfolds, David has an adulterous relationship with Bathsheba, gets her pregnant and then arranges to have her husband killed so he can be free to marry her.

But then, through the prophet Nathan, God confronts David with his sin, and David ends up spending several days and nights prostrate before the Lord, confessing his sin and repenting. And while there is no iron-clad connection between this episode in David's life and Psalm 51, theologians have traditionally believed that the prayer we read there is one of heartfelt confession and repentance for his double sin of adultery and murder described above.

Unlike Spitzer's "confession," David's prayer provides us with a model we can use when we need to confess our sins. David begins with these words:

Have mercy on me, O God,
> according to your unfailing love;
> according to your great compassion
> blot out my transgressions.
Wash away all my iniquity
> and cleanse me from my sin.
For I know my transgressions,
> and my sin is always before me.
Against you, you only, have I sinned
> and done what is evil in your sight,
> so that you are proved right when you speak
> and justified when you judge.
Surely I was sinful at birth,

sinful from the time my mother conceived me.
(Psalm 51:1–5)

The Fact of Sin

As we take a close look at David's prayer of confession, the first thing we notice is a completely unvarnished acknowledgement of his sin. He doesn't beat around the bush, call sin by some other name or attempt to downplay its seriousness. Instead, he calls his act a "transgression," a word that denotes rebellion against God's authority. He confesses, "Against you, you only, have I sinned and done what is evil in your sight." Remarkable, isn't it? Certainly there were other parties seriously hurt in this whole mess—Bathsheba and her husband, Uriah, for instance. But what dominates David's mind is that his sin was ultimately against God and God alone. That is true of every sin. While there may be (and usually is) horizontal fallout, we must deal first with the fact that sin is an act of rebellion against God. Not satisfied to label his act a transgression, David also refers to it as sin and iniquity ("wash away all my iniquity and cleanse me from my sin"). Iniquity carries the sense of a judicial liability the sinner bears for his actions, while "sin" is the violation of a standard. David's confession begins with a thorough and comprehensive acknowledgment of the fact of his sin as transgression, iniquity and sin. He calls it everything God says it is.

The Depth of Sin

Next David deals with the depth of his sin, going straight to the source in his confession: "Surely I was sinful at birth, sinful from the time my mother conceived me." What David is acknowledging here is that deep within there is a fundamental flaw in his makeup, a sin nature, inherent from the time he was conceived. This refers to the biblical doctrine of original sin. In contrast to the popular concept that we humans are good at heart but do wrong things once in a while, the Bible teaches that from birth we carry a built-in inclination to rebel against God, a bent toward transgression and crookedness in the very core of our being.

Anyone who has raised children can attest to the fact of original sin. Let me ask you: Did your parents have to teach you how to lie, how to throw a temper tantrum, how to blame other people? Why is it that we do not have to teach our children to do wrong, but we labor so diligently for years to teach them to do right? It is inside them from conception, just like it was in David. Swiss medical doctor Paul Tournier refers to this as the guilt of being. Specific sinful actions known as transgressions, iniquities and sin—the guilt of doing—flow from this fundamental guilt of being.

The Defilement of Sin

Having confessed the fact of his sin (calling it transgression, iniquity and sin) and its depth (inbred from the moment of conception), David proceeds to confess the defilement of his whole being by sin, though he couches this awareness of defilement in a passionate cry for a thorough scrubbing by God.

> Cleanse me with hyssop, and I will be clean;
>> wash me, and I will be whiter than snow.
> Let me hear joy and gladness;
>> let the bones you have crushed rejoice.

> Hide your face from my sins
> and blot out all my iniquity. (Psalm 51:7–9)

From reading this passage, it might be easy to conclude that *hyssop* was some kind of ancient cleansing agent, but it wasn't. It was a plant used in Israel's worship. Many of the sacrifices the priests offered for sin involved the shedding of blood. The priests would have to sprinkle the blood of the sacrifice upon the altar, and to do this they would fashion a brush from the leaves of the hyssop plant and use it to sprinkle the blood. So David in asking to be cleansed with hyssop is acknowledging that because of his sin, he has been defiled and thus rendered unfit for worship and for service of his God.

To get just a hint of his feeling of defilement, think back to an occasion when you unwittingly stepped on something soft and squishy, and within seconds, your nose confirmed your worst fears. Think of what followed: the furious attempts to wipe your soles on a nearby patch of grass, hurrying home and quickly shedding your shoes outside the door (until you get those filthy things off your feet, you feel unfit to enter), and the dread of having to wash those shoes. If only someone could do it for us—thoroughly—until every vestige of the offending material is expunged.

Tell me, when was the last time you felt that way about your sin? That is what David was feeling here. And as a defiled person, he felt unfit to worship so he cried for cleansing and washing. Only God can clean him "white as snow."

His subsequent cry for God to restore to him the former joy and gladness most likely refer, within the Old Testament context, to his joyful participation in the corporate worship life of his people. His request for God to hide His face from his sins is in fact a request that He would not hide His face from David—which implies loss of communion and intimacy with God. So all of verses 7–9 deal with this issue of defilement of sin that renders him unfit for glad worship in God's presence with God's people.

We need to follow David's example when we confess our sins. First we need to confess the *fact* of our sin thoroughly, calling it what God calls it—*transgression,* which is rebellion against divine authority, *iniquity* which leaves us liable and guilty, and *sin* which is crookedness, offense against a standard. Then we confess the *depth* of our sin, that the specific sin we have committed is rooted in a *sin nature* that is ours from conception. Finally we need to feel and confess the *defilement* of our sin that renders us *unfit* to worship and serve our God or enjoy His presence in any way. This paves the way for prayers for cleansing and restoration to intimacy with Him in worship and service.

What a dramatic contrast between David's opening words of confession and Spitzer's opening words about all the good he had done for the city of New York and the vision of progressive politics he had pursued for the last eight years.

Radical Renewal

Now precisely because David has dealt so thoroughly with the problem, he prays for the solution to be equally thorough as well. He moves from an unvarnished acknowledgment of what he has done to a desire for radical cleansing and renewal—something that David has no ability to muster on his own:

> Surely you desire truth in the inner parts;
>   you teach me wisdom in the inmost place. . . .
> Create in me a pure heart,
>   O God, and renew a steadfast spirit within me.
> Do not cast me from your presence
>   or take your Holy Spirit from me.
> Restore to me the joy of your salvation
>   and grant me a willing spirit, to sustain me.
>   (Psalm 51:10–12)

David focuses on the inner parts and the inmost place, using different words. First he acknowledges that God desires truth in the "inner part," which in the Old Testament is often interchangeable with "heart" and "spirit," referring to that central core of our being that spills over and affects everything. The writer of Proverbs 4:23 captures the sense of this inner part when he counsels, "Guard your heart, for it is the wellspring of life."

Next David refers to the wisdom that God teaches him "in the inmost place." The Hebrew word for "inmost" could also be rendered "secret," and it carries the idea of something that has been garrisoned and protected by many layers—a place that is hard to get at. So David is saying, in essence, "Because my problem is at the core of my being, the solution has to be at the core of my being and I can't get at it. Father, only You can, and You have to do it because You desire to place truth and wisdom there."

Then, just as he uses three different words for sin, he also uses three distinct phrases to describe what he wants God to do for him. First he prays, "Create in me a pure heart." The Hebrew word *bara*, translated "create," carries the idea of bringing something radically new into being. Another feature of *bara* is that it is used only with God as subject. David uses this same powerful word to beseech God, praying in essence, "At my physical birth something was wrong with me at the very core of my being that inclined me toward transgression, iniquity and sin. Thus, God, I need You to do a work of radical re-creation in the core of my being, something only You can do, so that I will now be naturally inclined to follow hard after You."

Next he asks God to "renew a steadfast spirit within me," and in using this word "steadfast," he is asking God to strengthen him supernaturally for a distinct task that is before him. In his transgression, David is painfully aware not only of his personal failing, but of his failure as king—a task to which God had raised and commissioned him. In that realization, he cries out: "Lord, I am Your anointed servant, Your divine representative on this earth, and I need You to strengthen me to be able to do this work properly as vice-regent and king. So God, give me a steadfast spirit."

Then David prays that God would grant him a "willing spirit." You see, it is possible to be steadfast, but do it all joylessly and out of a sense of duty. But what we know of David tells us that he would have none of that. His heart's cry is: "God, I want to have a willing spirit inside of me. Create something new in me so that my inclinations will be the exact opposite of my nature. Make me capable and strong to do this work that You have called me to do in Your kingdom, to represent You righteously, and change the very desires of my heart so that I will enjoy and delight in what You have called me to do."

David's next request warrants special consideration, because I believe that when he prays, "Do not cast me from your presence or take your Holy Spirit from me" (51:11), he is hearkening back to the terrible consequences of sin that befell his predecessor, Saul. In reading the tragic account of Saul's rise and fall, we see that the Spirit of God first came powerfully upon King Saul, but as a result of sin and disobedience to God's clear direction, the Spirit departed from Saul and an evil spirit came upon him instead (see 1 Samuel 16:14).

David was actually serving Saul during this time, and witnessed the results of this evil spirit in Saul's life (eventually driving him to witchcraft and suicide). We can well understand David's fear that because of his grievous sin, the same fate might befall him. So he prays, "You took Your spirit away from my predecessor for his sin and disobedience. But now, Lord, I beseech You not to take Your Holy Spirit away from me because of what I've done."

Restoration to Useful Ministry

Finally, because he has been so thorough in dealing with his sin and in asking for renewal, David is able to break through with confidence concerning the future.

> Then I will teach transgressors your ways,
>   and sinners will turn back to you.
> Save me from bloodguilt, O God,
>   the God who saves me,
>   and my tongue will sing of your righteousness.
> O Lord, open my lips,
>   and my mouth will declare your praise.
> You do not delight in sacrifice, or I would bring it;

you do not take pleasure in burnt offerings.
The sacrifices of God are a broken spirit;
    a broken and contrite heart,
    O God, you will not despise (Psalm 51:13–17).

Recall how he began, with a sense of defilement that had rendered him unfit for service and worship. Now he is saying, in effect, "God, not only are You going to cleanse me, but You are also going to make me useful in the kingdom of God once again." The first dimension of this confidence is that he will teach transgressors God's ways.

In context it must mean the way back to God from estrangement and defilement caused by one's sin. More specifically it will be the way that David took that begins with a thorough acknowledgment of the fact, depth and defilement of sin and a way that continues with a desire for radical cleansing and renewal at the very core of one's being—nothing less than a whole new creative work of the Holy Spirit.

The amazing thing is that for three thousand years, David has been doing precisely this as countless believers have been led back to fellowship with God after grievous sins through the wisdom contained in Psalm 51. Eliot Spitzer, meanwhile, is already forgotten, teaching nobody anything. David also expresses confidence that sinners will turn back to God. In other words, he is confident not only of a future teaching ministry, but a fruitful one at that.

David's confidence has nothing to do with negotiation, passing the buck or recounting all the good he has done as Israel's king. It is based totally on God's mercy and David's humble reception of His forgiveness, cleansing and renewal. We see this clearly in his opening words:

> Have mercy on me, O God,
>> according to your unfailing love;
>> according to your great compassion
>> blot out my transgressions. . . .
>
> Against you, you only, have I sinned
>> and done what is evil in your sight,
>> so that you are proved right when you speak
>> and justified when you judge. (Psalm 51:1, 4)

With no attempt at self-justification, David is saying, in effect, "God, You are the Judge, and if You refused my prayer for forgiveness, cleansing and restoration to ministry and instead judged me, You would be absolutely righteous in this. Nonetheless, I am calling upon Your unfailing love."

The Hebrew word for this "unfailing love" upon which David bases all his hope, is *hesed*, and while there is no straightforward English equivalent, it signifies loyalty to the terms of a covenant that a person makes with another party. It also signifies that the power to keep that covenant comes from within the person's own nature.

Let's put that in terms of God's covenant with each of us as believers: He has made a covenant with us in Jesus Christ, sealed by His blood. It is an unconditional, everlasting, unilateral covenant of grace. Thus, with David we can declare, "Lord, I am counting upon Your power to keep that covenant, a power I do not have. I am standing upon Your *hesed*—Your unfailing love—to forgive, renew and restore me."

Kick-Starting the Process

You might wonder what triggers the type of confession David models in Psalm 51 and how you can embrace that model in your own life. The basic answer is God's confrontational Word. In David's case, confession was prompted when God's Word, through his prophet, powerfully confronted David with his sin.

We witness this same pattern in the Apostle Paul's two letters to the Corinthian church. The first was confrontational, pointing out the various sins in their midst and the need for confession and repentance. And what was the result of that confrontation? The Holy Spirit worked strongly in the hearts of these believers, so that Paul could write in a subsequent epistle that he rejoiced because "your sorrow led to repentance. For you were made sorry in a godly manner, that you might suffer loss from us in nothing. For godly sorrow produces repentance *leading* to salvation, not to be regretted." (2 Corinthians 7:9–10, NKJV).

So it is today. The same Scriptures that give us fuel for worship prayer can become the Word of God that exposes our sin for what it is and precipitate a "Davidic" confession. This might happen as we are reading the Bible devotionally, listening to it expounded in a sermon, hearing it shared in a small-group Bible study or even while studying God's Word to teach it to others.

I recall many years ago teaching a Sunday school class on the book of Hebrews. One evening as I prepared a lesson, I read the passage in which the writer hearkens back to Israel's rebellion in the desert, quoting from Psalm 95: "Today, if you hear his voice, / do not harden your hearts / as you did in the rebellion" (Hebrews 3:15).

As I reflected on that verse, God hit me over the head with a spiritual sledgehammer, convicting me of the lack of consistent prayer in my life. This profound confrontation concerning my spiritual condition came directly through God's Word, and brought me to true confession, repentance and sustained obedience in the area of prayer.

Confession can also be prompted by self-examination, which means deliberately putting ourselves in a place where the Holy Spirit can test our hearts. It is a little like going to the doctor for an annual physical exam. You submit to all kinds of prodding and poking, not because something is necessarily wrong, but to determine the possible presence or beginning of a physical condition. In the same way, voluntary and deliberate spiritual self-examination can reveal sin that we need to deal with.

And just as with an annual physical exam, the calendar can help us here. For example, the church traditionally sets apart the season of Lent (the forty days prior to Easter) for believers to focus on the suffering of Christ and to examine their hearts. In many congregations this takes the form of corporate prayer and confession. In past eras of the church, men and women used a form of prayer called a *litany* to help them conduct a thorough self-examination.

One of the litanies I have used over the years is called the *Southwell Litany* written by the Rev. George Ridding, a bishop in the Church of England during the 1800s. Reading and reflecting on the confessions in this particular prayer is like having a spiritual doctor—specifically, the Holy Spirit—put His finger on problem areas. As you read the excerpts below, take a few moments to ask God to shine His light on potential areas in your own life that you may need to address:

> Lord, open our minds to see ourselves as you see us, or even as others see us and we see others;
> And from all unwillingness to know our infirmities,
> Save us and help us, O Lord.
>
> . . . .
>
> From pride and self-will, from the desire to have our own way in all things, from an overweening love of our own ideas and blindness to the value of others, from resentment against opposition and contempt for the claims of others:
> Enlarge the generosity of our hearts and enlighten the fairness of our judgments;
> And from all selfish arbitrariness of temper,
> Save us and help us, O Lord.
>
> From jealousy, whether of equals or superiors, from grudging others success, from impatience of submission and eagerness for authority:
> Give us the spirit of community to share loyally with fellow workers in all true proportions;
> And from all insubordination to just law and proper authority,
> Save us and help us, O Lord.
>
> . . . .
>
> From strife, partisanship, and division, from magnifying our certainties to condemn all differences, from building our systems to exclude all challenges, and from all arrogance in our dealings with others,
>
> Save us and help us, O Lord.[2]

Left to ourselves, how likely is it that we would have prayed with such depth of insight into our hearts?

Don't quit this practice of self-examination—ever!

Radical confession of sin and prayer for equally radical cleansing and renewal are the only right responses to conviction of sin—but they are no guarantee that we will not commit that sin again. The Apostle Paul tells us that the battles we fight are not against flesh and blood, but "against the rulers, against the authorities, against the powers of this dark world and against the spiritual forces of evil in the heavenly realms" (Ephesians 6:12).

These enemies don't give up ground without a struggle, one that can sometimes take months, years, even decades to win. We will go through repeated cycles of failure, followed by deep, thoroughgoing confession and restoration. The key is perseverance, refusing to quit. In his book *Eros Defiled,* John White writes about this, and though he is specifically referring to sexual sins, what he says applies to any sin and the need to persevere in defeating it:

> Thank God . . . for the day when you will be master of your [desires]. Though it tarry, it will come, as you let God be master in other areas of your life. . . . By all means groan, but take your shame to the throne of grace where blood will wash it away. . . . Thomas R. Kelly said, "Humility does not rest . . . upon bafflement and discouragement and self-disgust at our shabby lives or a brow-beaten, dog-slinking attitude. It rests upon the disclosure of the consummate wonder of God." He also says, "When you catch yourself again, *lose no time in self-recriminations,* but breathe a silent prayer of forgiveness and begin again just where you are." [3]

White summarizes his advice with this bold statement: "Learn to laugh at your chains, in faith." Whoever is serious about confessing his sins, as David was, can learn to laugh at the enemy's efforts to put chains on us and continue to persevere until God breaks them completely.

Questions for Group Study

1. Read the quote from Elliot Spitzer and compare it to Luke 18:10–14. Leaving any political views aside, and acknowledging that Spitzer's words were a public statement and not a prayer to God, are there any similarities? What does the passage in Luke teach us about confession?

2. Reread Psalm 51:1–5 and try to identify within the prayer the three points mentioned by the author: the fact of sin, the depth of sin, and the defilement of sin.

3. What does the author mean by "radical renewal"? What is our part in this process? What is God's part?

4. Discuss the importance of Scripture in bringing about repentance and confession such as is found in David's prayer and among the church in Corinth (see 2 Corinthians 7:9–10). Share an instance in your life when you were impacted in this way by God's Word.

5. What is the role of self-examination in the life of a Christian? Discuss the value and/or drawbacks of observing specific times of self-examination such as Lent, as well as the use of litany prayer.

6. What does John White mean when he counsels us to "learn to laugh at your chains, in faith"? Conclude the discussion with a time of prayer for victory over "besetting sins"; perhaps your group is one in which you can freely practice the biblical advice to "confess your faults one to another, and pray one for another, that ye may be healed" (James 5:16 KJV).

Chapter 7

Fellowship: Sharing Our Lives

If you were to ask the average Christ-follower to sketch out a spiritual map that would most effectively lead one to maturity in Christ, he or she would likely include most if not all of the spiritual disciplines we have studied thus far as signposts on that journey. Certainly, as we have already argued, the disciplines of worship, Scripture reading, study, prayer and confession are all vital links in our relationship with God. They are the sails we must learn to hoist to catch the wind of the Spirit.

But what about those disciplines with a horizontal focus which help form Christ in us through our interactions and relationships with other people? While fewer believers might recognize the importance of fellowship, service and giving in bringing us to maturity in Christ, these three people-centered disciplines are vital in our quest to harness the motive power of the Holy Spirit.

In his book *Christ Plays in Ten Thousand Places,* respected theologian and veteran pastor Eugene H. Peterson recalls his transition from the academic world, where he had served as a seminary professor, to that of full-time pastor. The change was not as easy as you might think, and it led him to eventually acknowledge the critical role of community in spiritual formation:

> When I became a pastor, I didn't think much about the complexities of community in general and of a holy community in particular; I was absorbed in the theatrical glories of creation and the dramatic workings of salvation in history. I was moving from city to city, going from school to school. I was given gatherings of people to study with, work with, play with—but it was all fairly transient. And then it no longer was transient—this was it. A congregation, improbably named the people of God. These people for good or ill, but *these* people. I often found myself preferring the company of people outside my congregation, men and women who did not follow Jesus. Or worse, preferring the company of my sovereign self. But I soon found that my preferences were honored by neither Scripture nor Jesus.
>
> I didn't come to the conviction easily, but finally there was no getting around it: There can be no maturity in the spiritual life, no obedience in following Jesus, no wholeness in the Christian life apart from an immersion and embrace of community. I am not myself by myself. Community, not the highly vaunted individualism of our culture, is the setting in which Christ is at play.[1]

Casseroles, Anyone?

I recall reading about a Sunday school teacher who asked the children in her class to bring something the following week that they believed symbolized the church. One child brought a cross, another one a Bible, but the unexpected arrived with one child who brought a casserole. His reason? "My mother is always bringing casseroles to church."

That casserole, I believe, is a very appropriate metaphor for the most common understanding of fellowship. The word is almost exclusively used in Western evangelical circles to denote activities that a congregation typically pursues outside the confines of regular worship services. Many churches have what is referred to as a "fellowship hall," which is used for Sunday "potluck" dinners, ice cream socials, baby showers, youth get-togethers, wedding receptions and other sundry "fellowship" events. What pastor hasn't found himself inviting the congregation to "join us after the service for a time of fellowship," meaning people getting together for cookies, coffee and lighthearted conversation?

There is nothing wrong with this kind of activity, but it is only a very small part of what the Bible calls fellowship—and it is by no means the most important part. Fellowship with other believers is a specific spiritual discipline and one we must cultivate and pursue intentionally.

We first encounter New Testament fellowship in Acts 2. After Christ's ascension, His disciples wait in the Upper Room until Pentecost, when they are filled with the Holy Spirit and propelled out into the busy streets thronging with pilgrims from all over the known world.

Peter explains the significance of this outpouring of the Spirit as the fulfillment of the promise of an Old Testament prophet, Joel.

He then proceeds to preach Jesus—His life, death, resurrection and ascension, leading to this coming of the Spirit. About three thousand individuals are convicted of their need for salvation; they receive Jesus as Savior and Lord, are baptized, and the church is born.

What happens next gives us insight into true fellowship:

> They devoted themselves to the apostles' teaching and to the fellowship, to the breaking of bread and to prayer. Everyone was filled with awe, and many wonders and miraculous signs were done by the apostles. All the believers were together and had everything in common. Selling their possessions and goods, they gave to anyone as he had need. Every day they continued to meet together in the temple courts. They broke bread in their homes and ate together with glad and sincere hearts, praising God and enjoying the favor of all the people. And the Lord added to their number daily those who were being saved.
> (Acts 2:42–47)

The Greek word used here for fellowship is *koinonia,* translated in several places in the New Testament as "share," "sharing," "participate," "participation" or "holding things in common," as in the Acts passage above. One of the most concrete demonstrations of this *koinonia* was a selfless attitude toward material possessions. Everyone considered what they had as belonging not just to them but to the whole community, and they made it available to others as needed.

This was not a merely temporary generosity brought on by the euphoria of the moment. Some time later, when the church began to experience persecution because of the gospel, they came together in prayer and God once again poured out His Spirit. Notice the believers' response:

> All the believers were one in heart and mind. No one claimed that any of his possessions was his own, but they shared everything they had. . . . There were no needy persons among them. For from time to time those who owned lands or houses sold them, brought the money from the sales and put it at the apostles' feet, and it was distributed to anyone as he had need. (Acts 4:32, 34–35)

Voluntary Oneness, Not Socialism

Many people have wrongly concluded from this account that the early church did not believe in private ownership of property. On the contrary, this text clearly says that people *owned* homes and lands and sold them from time to time, at their own initiative. In the very next chapter, we read the story of a man who voluntarily sold some property but gave only part of the money while pretending to give it all. Notice that when the Apostle Peter confronted the man, it was not for keeping back part of the money, but for deception: "Didn't it belong to you before it was sold? And after it was sold, wasn't the money at your disposal? What made you think of doing such a thing? You have not lied to men but to God" (Acts 5:4).

What characterized the early church was not the abandonment of private ownership of property, but such a sense of oneness, of belonging to one another, that they could live out the mind-set of "what's mine is yours when you need it." That's true fellowship: the heartfelt sense of belonging to one another to such an extent that what we have is freely available to other believers when they need help.

And it is not restricted to sharing money and other possessions. Money is simply an obvious and concrete expression of the "what's mine is yours" attitude. Frankly, in today's prosperous society, we might actually find it easier to give our money than our time, our attention, our heartfelt encouragement, or our simple presence in the lives of someone in the throes of pain and suffering.

Finally, this text also says they were devoted to fellowship. "Devoted" carries the idea of persevering or continuing steadfast in something. The members of the early church were not "dabbling" in fellowship; they continued steadfastly in this heart attitude of belonging to one another to the extent that "what's mine is yours." What a radical contrast to "casserole Christianity"; how vastly beyond food, fun and "nice" conversation in the fellowship hall!

Fellowship in the Trenches

This concept of true fellowship among believers applies as much to a group of three believers as it does to three thousand. Let's fast-forward to twenty years after the birth of the New Testament church where we find the Apostle Paul strongly encouraging a Christ-follower by the name of Philemon to be generous in his relationship with Onesimus, a brother in Christ. The interesting wrinkle in this story is that not only is Onesimus a fellow believer, but he is also Philemon's slave—and a runaway slave at that! In those ancient times, it was customary for people to keep slaves, and it was not unheard of for slaves to run away for a variety of reasons. If a runaway slave was caught, his master could put him to death without answering to anybody since the slave was considered the master's property.

Evidently Onesimus went to Rome, crossed paths with Paul, heard the gospel and became a Christ-follower. In befriending him, Paul discovers that he is a runaway slave who belongs to another Christian brother, Philemon. Paul's wise counsel to Onesimus is, "You must go back to your master."

This new believer must have found Paul's advice terrifying, given the possible consequences he could face upon his return. But Paul assures him, "I know your master and I will send along a letter on your behalf." That letter we know as the Epistle of Paul to Philemon, and it allows us to get to the heart of what true fellowship in Christ—this *koinonia*—is all about.

> I then, as Paul . . . appeal to you for my son Onesimus, who became my son while I was in chains. Formerly he was useless to you, but now he has become useful both to you and to me. I am sending him—who is my very heart—back to you. . . . Perhaps the reason he was separated from you for a little while was that you might have him back for good—no longer as a slave, but better than a slave, as a dear brother. He is very dear to me but even dearer to you, both as a man and as a brother in the Lord. So if you consider me a partner, welcome him as you would welcome me. If he has done you any wrong or owes you anything, charge it to me. I, Paul, am writing this with my own hand. I

will pay it back—not to mention that you owe me your very self. (Philemon 1:9–12, 15–19)

Consider especially Paul's words in verses 17 and 18: "So if you consider me a partner, welcome him as you would welcome me. If he has done you any wrong or owes you anything, charge it to me." That word *partner* is derived from the same word—*koinonia*. Paul is saying, in effect, "Philemon, if you have the kind of heart connection with me so that what's yours is mine when I need it and what's mine is yours when you need it, then please welcome Onesimus back the same way you would welcome me. What you feel about me is the way you should feel about Onesimus because he is now part of the same fellowship by virtue of his conversion to Christ."

He proceeds to reinforce this attitude when he tells Philemon to charge to him, Paul, whatever Onesimus owes him. Why? Because Paul and Onesimus are totally interchangeable in Paul's eyes, so closely identified are they with one another in this *koinonia*. It is clear that the basis of Paul's appeal to Philemon to take Onesimus back is the deep sharing, the mutual participation in Christ to the extent of mutual identification with one another. It is the fellowship in the church of three thousand in Acts 2, played out in a very different setting twenty years later among three believers.

Earlier in this same letter, Paul draws attention to the fact that Philemon is already practicing true fellowship, for Paul writes:

I always thank my God as I remember you in my prayers, because I hear about your faith in the Lord Jesus and your love for all the saints. I pray that you

may be active in sharing your faith, so that you will
have a full understanding of every good thing we
have in Christ. Your love has given me great joy and
encouragement, because you, brother, have refreshed
the hearts of the saints. (1:4–7)

But in verse 6, stuck right in the middle of his praise
of Philemon, Paul adds that he is praying that "you may
be active in sharing your faith, so that you will have
a full understanding of every good thing we have in
Christ." This verse is often used in sermons on evangelism and encouragement to share one's faith, but this is
to wrench the verse out of context. The "sharing" that
Paul is encouraging Philemon to do has nothing to do
with witnessing. This word used here is the now-familiar
koinonia! What Paul is actually saying to Philemon is
along these lines: "I am praying that God will enable you
to see your former slave Onesimus in a new way so that
you will receive him back like you would receive me and
experience in yourself the active working of the good-
ness of God that is building up the community, the body
of Christ."

Long-Haul Relationships

In Philemon we see a Christ-follower who is already
doing well in the area of fellowship (Paul commends his
refreshing love for all the saints). Yet Paul prays that he
will take it one step further. That's why fellowship is also
a spiritual discipline. It is not only the amazing creation
of the Holy Spirit; it is also the means by which we grow.

That naturally leads to the question, "How exactly
does fellowship transform us?" For me, a helpful starting point in answering this question was to look at those

relationships that have really made me grow. The most obvious one that came to mind right away was marriage. Next I thought of my relationship with my children and my commitment over the years to do my part in transmitting the faith to them. And then I thought of the thirty-nine years I had been in relationship with one local church. Those relationships have contributed more to my growth than any other.

And they all have one thing in common: Every one has been, and continues to be, a long-term commitment; moreover, in the first two, marriage and parenting, there is no way out without being disobedient to God. (Even a church cannot be "dumped" by a pastor for purely personal reasons; the longer he has been in that church, the more crucial this becomes.)

Precisely because of the permanency of these relationships, I had to change and grow; the alternative was to be mired in mediocrity at best and, at worst, reap a harvest of bitterness and suffering down the line. What, then, of those who are single or childless or have had to change churches for various legitimate reasons? Is growth through true fellowship out of the question for them? Not at all. They are but three illustrations of the general principle that true and lasting fellowship—*koinonia*—can only happen where there is ongoing commitment to one another in long-haul relationships, in which individuals are on a common mission and hang with each other through the highs and lows of life.

Paul is referring to just such relationships when he writes, "I thank my God every time I remember you. In all my prayers for all of you, I always pray with joy because of your partnership in the gospel from the first day until now" (Philippians 1:3–5). The word Paul uses for "partnership" is—once again—*koinonia,* and there is no more worthy a mission in which God's people can partner than in spreading the gospel. Such fellowship may work itself out as we partner with fellow believers in evangelizing our own communities and neighborhoods; at the same time, it may cast a wider net as we partner with those spreading the gospel around the world.

An illustration from my own life might help show how this works out in practice. One day, while working on a sermon that formed the basis of this chapter, I took a break and went out to "prayer walk" a ravine near the church. I took along with me a prayer letter from an international worker associated with our church who was teaching in a school for missionary children in a limited-access nation.

As I read her account of what God was doing in the life of the high school students, I grew. How? My picture of God grew larger, my prayers grew more passionate, my vision and desire for God to do similar things for our own young people got stoked, my excitement at my own calling to keep the missionary vision alive before my congregation got fired up, and so on. As I read the letter, her struggles and needs became mine—I experienced *koinonia,* the interchangeability of one another in the body. These shared feelings deepened as I continued to pray. That's one way in which relationships built around a common mission help us grow.

Fellowship and Submission

A second category of relationships that cause us to

grow are relationships that require submission. The Apostle Paul addresses this issue throughout his epistles, pointing out the need for us to submit to one another (see Ephesians 5:21) as well as to those who exercise authority in our lives (see Hebrews 13:17). While submitting to authorities can refer to those in our government or our place of employment, in a local church context— which is what I want to address here—it means willingly placing ourselves under the protective and disciplining authority of the elders in leadership in our individual congregations.

In our increasingly fragmented and rebellious society, the idea of submitting to authority can rankle some people. But in the church, there is simply no other way to enjoy the blessings of a fruitful life in the kingdom of God. Such submission does not mean mindlessly surrendering to the unreasonable agendas of strong-willed authoritarians. That being said, humble submission to God-appointed spiritual authority is a place where true spiritual growth can take place and where our mistakes and missteps can be corrected in a safe and understanding environment.

As a pastor, I have had the privilege of seeing this firsthand on several occasions. Once, the elders in our church were called upon to publicly discipline someone in a leadership position who was guilty of a transgression in the area of business ethics. This individual could have taken the easy way out, refused correction and left the church. Instead, he humbled himself to receive the needed correction, repented of his wrong and willingly met with two elders every week for one full year.

He remains a textbook example to the entire congregation of what true submission in the context of fellowship is all about. Instead of reacting in pride and anger, justifying his behavior and leaving a wreckage of ruined relationships and regrets, he simply submitted himself to the discipline of the elders, with the result that healing came on many levels, opening the door to the continued blessing of God in his life and family. A submissive relationship helped him grow.

Of course, submission to spiritual authority is not only for discipline and correction. In its most positive sense, it is played out as younger believers voluntarily submit to the spiritual wisdom and authority of those who are further along in the faith. Not long ago I witnessed a great example of this in our own congregation when I happened upon a young lady waiting to meet with her mentor, another lady in our church. In the course of a short conversation, I asked who her mentor was and found that it wasn't someone many years older than she was, but someone in her own age group who happened to be a little ahead of her in spiritual maturity, and who had agreed to pour what she knew into the life of this young believer. This, you see, is the real definition of fellowship—connecting with others in life-transforming relationships that will bear fruit for eternity.

In his powerfully personal book *Rebuilding Your Broken World,* written after a moral failure prompted him to reevaluate his life and priorities, Gordon MacDonald notes:

> In the environment of ambition, the desire to establish oneself and one's dreams, there is the greater likelihood of compromise. The desire to establish a career, get a foothold in an organization, might make

it easier for one to turn one's head in the moment of an unethical decision or to ignore an injustice being done to a fellow worker. "Making waves," as some put it, is not the most judicious thing when you're young and vulnerable in the marketplace. There's always someone ready to step in and take your place, one hears. Pressure mounts and a person finds it much easier to take the first steps toward choices and decisions never before thought possible.

These are just a few reasons why young adults badly need mentors or sponsors, older couples who come alongside and offer supportive wisdom, encouragement and models of godly behavior. Young adults can thrive in these difficult environments when they renounce the youthful tendency to want to go it alone and seek relationships providing guidance and accountability. In no other phase of life is it more important to establish clear, routine spiritual disciplines than in young adulthood. The temptation to rely on abundant energy, youthful charisma, and inner enthusiasm will lead many to ignore the necessity of quiet, solitude, reflection, and listening. And that temptation has to be checked and countered with the prayerful and receptive lifestyle. In these ways the danger points in the environment are all but neutralized.[2]

Peer Relationships

When you get right down to it, the people you inter-act with the most at church are not your leaders or men-tors. They are, instead, your peers, and these are by and large the ones with whom you are called to pursue true fellowship. They are the ones of whom the Apostle Paul counsels us, "Submit to one another out of reverence for

Christ" (Ephesians 5:21). What does submitting to one another look like, and how do we do it successfully?

In the academic world, before you can publish a research study or some other paper, you must submit to a process called "peer review." This means your work must be subjected to the critical eye of others working in your field who make it their responsibility to check out your research to make sure it all adds up. Work that is not subjected to peer review will lack credibility. While peer review might at times be painful, it is a necessary process, one that individuals within the academic world submit to for their own good.

In the same way, when it comes to what we believe, our take on Scripture, and other aspects of our walk with God, our peers in Christ are often our greatest allies and defense against error, and we need to welcome their active involvement in our lives. A classic example of how submitting to one another can play out occurred not long ago in our church.

A couple in the church was facing a major decision in life that involved a significant outlay of money and a temporary relocation that would cause a major disruption in their normally stable family. A young child was involved. The negative impact on their lives could be enormous if they made the wrong decision. So they wrote letters to several close friends at church ("fearless truth tellers," they called them), asking for unvarnished counsel and feedback.

They didn't have to submit to this "peer review" from their brothers and sisters in Christ, but they were glad they did, and deeply grateful for the wise and prayerful advice—along with brutally honest questions that probed motivation, ambition and obedience issues. Their friends, who loved them and wanted them to make the right decision, were willing to ask these questions and challenge some of their assumptions, so that when this couple finally made their decision, it was done with a multitude of godly counsel (see Proverbs 15:22).

Working together in teams—staff, boards, committees—is another aspect of peer relationships that provides opportunities for growth in Christlikeness. One mark of a good team is that people are different from, and complement, one another. Every time I sit down to a staff meeting in my church, I am amazed at how radically different each of us is from one another—and at how those differences usually enable a dynamic fruitfulness that otherwise would simply not be possible. Because each person in the group is different—in the way he thinks, in his skills and talents, in his perspectives—very seldom do we miss an important "take" on the agenda item of the moment.

But these same differences also have a potential for irritation, even conflict. Such conflict is not necessarily bad and should not automatically be avoided. I recall a speaker pointing out that "commitment plus conflict equals change." As we work in teams with people equally gifted but very different from us, we get the opportunity to learn the cardinal character qualities of humility, meekness and patience. Not surprisingly, we also discover that we are inclined to be proud rather than humble when things don't go our way, angry rather than meek when our rights are violated, and impatient and irritable rather than longsuffering when a discussion drags on.

Confession—On the Horizontal Plane

Mention of sins like pride, unjustified anger and impatience leads to perhaps one of the most important aspects of committed relationships that leads to growth—confession of our true spiritual state. We have already looked at confession in its vertical dimension in Chapter Six; here I want us to consider confession in the horizontal dimension.

As on a few other occasions that I have already noted earlier in the book, God handed me a perfect illustration of the practice of horizontal confession the very week that I was preparing a sermon that ended up shaping this chapter. It involved one of our elders, and I shared it in my sermon not only with his permission but at his suggestion.

At our monthly board meeting, we usually begin with a time of sharing. At this particular meeting, we asked ourselves the following question: "Where is God at work in your life, and what is happening?" Several shared encouraging reports, especially about the Sunday evening Bible study. Then one elder spoke up and said, "I have to tell you that I cannot share anything positive. The Sunday evening study has been doing nothing for me, and I am going through a spell of spiritual dryness."

He was practicing many of the spiritual disciplines covered in this book but felt he was simply going through the motions. Group members prayed for him. The next day he called me. Because of the flexibility in his work situation, he had decided not to go into work that day but instead set aside the whole morning to pray. God met him during this time and showed him that the dryness he was going through was a significant part of the Spirit's preparation for the preaching assignment he had that weekend.

When I met him on Sunday morning in church, he reported that his joy and enthusiasm were back. A few days later I asked him to once again recount the details of his experience to me and to "unpack" his feelings as he went through the process so I could accurately report this to the congregation as part of my sermon. This is what he told me:

"First of all, it was very difficult for me to share something negative, given that the whole flow of the sharing to that point had been positive. Second, my reluctance to share about my spiritual dryness was, I suspect, a desire to 'manage my image.' But once I did share, I experienced a huge sense of relief by getting it out in the open and by the way I was accepted by the others. Their acceptance was communicated by their prayers, not just for me, but for others around the table who were also going through difficult situations."

As for his preaching assignment that weekend, the feedback he got from the congregation about the relevance of his message was overwhelming. We can only guess what might have been the outcome in his personal life and ministry if, out of fear or for the sake of "managing his image," he had kept quiet. No coffee, cookies, casseroles or easy conversation in the "fellowship" hall could have done what that honest confession of the dryness of his soul and the resulting heartfelt prayers of his colleagues did.

First and Second Things

What fellowship really boils down to is the willingness for each of us to lay down our lives—our own agendas and desires—and in humility consider others' needs. Paul puts it this way in his epistle to the Philippians: "Do nothing out of selfish ambition or vain conceit, but in humility consider others better than yourselves. Each of you should look not only to your own interests, but also to the interests of others" (Philippians 2:3–4). In other words, he adds, "Your attitude should be the same as that of Christ Jesus" (2:5).

In Galatians 6:2, Paul refers to this ministry of bearing one another's burdens as fulfilling the "law of Christ"—whether the burden is sin that needs to be dealt with in a gentle and restorative manner (which Paul addresses in the very first verse of this chapter), financial hardships that need assistance, mentoring to bring young believers to maturity or oneness in the mission of Christ with those who have answered His call to live out the gospel in another culture.

I close with C.S. Lewis' wise "doctrine" regarding first and second things: Put first things first, he said, and second things will also have meaning. Put second things first and you lose both. I love my six grandchildren and also love photographing them. So long as I value my grandchildren over photographing them, I am likely to keep enjoying both. If my photography ever becomes of first importance, I stand to lose my joy in both. So practice true *koinonia* and you will find coffee and cookies in the fellowship hall meaningful. Make them the main thing and not only will you tire of them, you will have also lost the transforming power, and hence the joy, of *koinonia*.

Questions for Group Study

1. What do you think comes to the mind of most Christians when they hear the word *fellowship*? What is the author's definition, and how does it differ from the popular understanding of the word?

2. Read Acts 2:42–47 and 4:32–35 (the word translated "common" is *koinonia,* or "fellowship"). How could "fellowship" as seen in the first-century church be put into practice today?

3. The author uses the story of the slave Onesimus in Paul's letter to Philemon to bring out another aspect of fellowship. What can we learn about the nature of true fellowship from this letter?

4. The author asks the question, "How exactly does fellowship transform us?" How would you answer that question? How have you been changed by your relationships in the body of Christ? How have you changed others?

5. Read Hebrews 10:24 and discuss how you might be able to develop and improve your opportunities for growth through mentoring and being mentored, and through spiritual "peer review," as described in the chapter.

6. Part of fellowship, the author contends, is confessing our sins and failures to one another. How does honest and open confession to fellow believers lead us to grow in Christ's image? Do you have a fellow believer with whom you can be this transparent?

Chapter 8

Service

"No vital Christianity is possible unless at least three aspects of it are developed," wrote a godly Christian leader of years gone by. "These are the inner life of devotion, the outer life of service, and the intellectual life of rationality." [1]

The spiritual disciplines of worship, Scripture reading and meditation, prayer and confession help us cultivate a rich inner life of devotion. The discipline of study addresses the need for an intellectual life of rationality. In this chapter, we want to look at the outer life of service. It builds on the spiritual discipline of fellowship, which in fact provides the primary context for service.

One of the common preoccupations many Christians seem to face today is discerning God's will for their lives. Life in this modern world can be complex, throwing up a whole host of situations that require specific

wisdom and guidance from God. Career paths, relationship issues, questions of where one should live and even
what ministry endeavors one should be involved in—all
of these and many more require divine insight or direction.

But in this legitimate preoccupation with the logistics
of life, there is a real danger that we will completely lose
sight of the fact that the bulk of God's will for us has
been clearly revealed in Scripture—specifically that we
use the gifts He has given us to serve the body of Christ.
One of the foundational passages for gaining a clear
understanding of this dimension of service is found in
Romans 12, where the Apostle Paul writes:

> Therefore, I urge you, brothers, in view of God's
> mercy, to offer your bodies as living sacrifices, holy
> and pleasing to God—this is your spiritual act of
> worship. Do not conform any longer to the pattern
> of this world, but be transformed by the renewing of
> your mind. Then you will be able to test and approve
> what God's will is—his good, pleasing and perfect
> will. For by the grace given me I say to every one
> of you: Do not think of yourself more highly than
> you ought, but rather think of yourself with sober
> judgment, in accordance with the measure of faith
> God has given you. Just as each of us has one body
> with many members, and these members do not all
> have the same function, so in Christ we who are many
> form one body, and each member belongs to all the
> others. We have different gifts, according to the grace
> given us. If a man's gift is prophesying, let him use it in
> proportion to his faith. If it is serving, let him serve; if
> it is teaching, let him teach; if it is encouraging, let him
> encourage; if it is contributing to the needs of others,

let him give generously; if it is leadership, let him
govern diligently; if it is showing mercy, let him do it
cheerfully. (12:1–8)

God's Plan of Salvation

This passage begins with the word "therefore" because Paul is about to deal with the practical implications of all that he has covered in the preceding eleven
chapters. It is important for us to understand that these
preceding chapters comprise one of the clearest, most
exhaustive explanations of God's plan of salvation that
you will find in all the New Testament.

It is in these chapters that we read that all of us have
fallen short of the glory of God and are under His righteous judgment. It is here that Paul clearly lays out the
doctrine of justification by faith in Christ through His
death on the cross. It is here that we learn about sancti-
fication, the process by which we become increasingly
holy or "set apart" for God. It is in these chapters that we
read about the rich destiny that awaits us in the glori-
fication of our created bodies—something that all of
inanimate creation is waiting for "with bated breath." In
Romans 9, 10 and 11, Paul writes by inspiration of the
Holy Spirit about the mystery of Israel and how God's
Word has not failed, even though His chosen people
have rejected His great offer of salvation in Christ.

Paul concludes his truly awesome exposition of God's
plan of salvation with this magnificent doxology:

Oh, the depth of the riches of the wisdom and
    knowledge of God!
  How unsearchable his judgments,
  and his paths beyond tracing out!

"Who has known the mind of the Lord?
    Or who has been his counselor?"
"Who has ever given to God,
    that God should repay him?"
For from him and through him and to him are all
    things.
    To him be the glory forever! Amen.
(Romans 11:33–36)

"Present Your Bodies . . ."

Suddenly, seemingly without any warning, Paul follows up this magnificent exposition of the plan of salvation in all its past, present and future glory with an eminently practical, down-to-earth exhortation, admonishing us to "offer your bodies as living sacrifices, holy and pleasing to God," which he calls a "spiritual act of worship."

The first thing that many of us will ask is: What does it mean to be a "living sacrifice"? Paul offers a clear answer, explaining that as believers we are called to use the members of our bodies to serve one another. He points out that as members of the body of Christ, each of us belongs to one another, and our gifts and callings in His kingdom are meant to enrich and serve one another.

That's why I asserted earlier that service is an extension of the discipline of fellowship that we learned about in the last chapter. Remember, the essence of fellowship is a deep sense of connectedness to other Christ-followers, so that what I have and what I am belong to you, and what you have and are belong to me. This is true specifically of the spiritual gifts God has given each one of us.

Paul also says that our service to others through the use of these gifts is an act of worship that is pleasing to God. We tend to think of worship in a narrowly focused corridor of singing, prayer and praise, while God sees worship in a much broader way that includes pouring out all we have and are to the service of His body. So whether you are standing in the pulpit preaching, playing an instrument and leading others in singing, ushering, serving in the nursery or cleaning the church during the week—the ways we serve the body of Christ are nearly endless—you are engaged in a "spiritual act of worship" that is "holy and pleasing to God."

It is crucial for us to understand that worship involves both the sense of God and the service of God. We respond to His presence both privately and corporately through the more obvious acts of worship like singing, verbalizing our praise and declaring His Word. Out of this heartfelt worship flows the active worship of service that we engage in throughout our lives. It is a total self-contradiction to leave a corporate service claiming to have had a wonderful time of worship, only to be totally disengaged throughout the week from serving the body of Christ through the gifts God has given us.

Precisely because our service to one another is an act of worship, having the right attitude when using our spiritual gifts is critical. In Romans 12:1–8 Paul tells us to give generously, govern diligently and show mercy cheerfully. The ways in which we exercise the spiritual gifts (generously, diligently, cheerfully) become as important as the gifts themselves. In Malachi, God dealt strongly with those of His people who offered Him blemished and second-best sacrifices:

"When you bring blind animals for sacrifice, is that not wrong? When you sacrifice crippled or diseased animals, is that not wrong? Try offering them to your governor! Would he be pleased with you? Would he accept you?" says the LORD Almighty. . . . "Oh, that one of you would shut the temple doors, so that you would not light useless fires on my altar! I am not pleased with you," says the LORD Almighty, "and I will accept no offering from your hands. My name will be great among the nations, from the rising to the setting of the sun. In every place incense and pure offerings will be brought to my name, because my name will be great among the nations," says the LORD Almighty. "But you profane it by saying of the Lord's table, 'It is defiled,' and of its food, 'It is contemptible.' And you say, 'What a burden!' and you sniff at it contemptuously," says the LORD Almighty. (Malachi 1:8, 10–13)

If leftovers were totally unacceptable to God when it came to dead sacrifices, what would He have to say about "leftover" living sacrifices—giving less than our best when serving one another in the body through our spiritual gifts? That is basically giving leftovers and is equally unacceptable to God.

Good, Perfect and Pleasing

Given that wholehearted and excellent service through our spiritual gifts is a huge part of God's will for our lives and is at the same time an act of worship, it becomes important for us to get a good handle on our gifts. That is why Paul counsels in this passage, "Do not think of yourself more highly than you ought, but rather think of yourself with sober judgment." In other words, we need to be careful and deliberate in getting an accurate appraisal of what our gifts to the body are—and what they are not. Then we will be perfectly positioned to determine God's good, pleasing and perfect will.

The Greek word used here for "perfect" doesn't mean a flawless and trouble-free experience. The word here actually comes from the Greek word *teleios,* which carries the meaning of "end" as in "intended purpose." In other words, when you are in God's perfect will, you will find yourself involved in those things *for which God created you.* You will get that unique sense of satisfaction that comes from doing what you have been made to do. When you are in that place, you will find yourself thinking, *This is good, this is pleasing, this is what I have been made for.* With Eric Liddell of *Chariots of Fire* fame, you will say, "I feel His pleasure when I use my gifts in this way."

What Pastors Should Be Doing

One crucial implication of Paul's exhortation to find and use our gifts is the key role of pastors in local churches. Have you ever wondered what ought to be included in a pastor's job description? I am not referring to all the things we think our pastor should do to keep us happy, but rather the things he should be doing according to the mandate of Scripture. Paul addresses this head-on in Ephesians 4 when he writes:

> But to each one of us grace has been given as Christ apportioned it. . . . It was he who gave some to be apostles, some to be prophets, some to be evangelists, and some to be pastors and teachers, to prepare God's people for works of service, so that the body of Christ may be built up until we all reach unity in the faith and in the knowledge of the Son of God and become

mature, attaining to the whole measure of the fullness of Christ. (4:7, 11–13)

Notice that in speaking of spiritual gifts, Paul says, "To each one of us grace has been given." The gifts God bestows upon us to serve others are not meant to be burdensome, but an experience of His grace. So when it comes to service, our response need not be, "Oh no! I have to serve people," but rather, "I am about to experience His good, pleasing and perfectly suited blessing."

Note also that there are two kinds of gifts Paul is referring to here. The first kind is the offices of ministry, which he identifies as apostles, prophets, evangelists, pastors and teachers. You ought to consider the pastoral staff in your church as God's gifts to you. (It would be sheer arrogance for me, as a pastor, to say this if the Bible didn't clearly affirm that it is indeed so.)

These ministry offices are given by God to equip and prepare His people for the works of service to which they are called so that the body of Christ will be built up. These works of service are the second kind of gift Paul is talking about. In other words, the primary job description of your pastor, according to the Apostle Paul, is to equip *you*—to put the right tools in your hands and train you how to use them—so that you can then bless the rest of us in the body, which will in turn be built up into maturity, into the fullness of Christ.

How different this is from the mind-set in many churches where the pastor is considered to be little more than an instrument to meet the "felt needs" of the congregation! Of course, those who aren't satisfied customers will quickly move on to some other church to try to find what they want.

In sharp contrast to this consumer mentality, you ought to have the mind-set that says, "I am going to pray diligently for the leadership in my church so that they'll be committed to equipping and training me to use the spiritual gifts God has given me so I can do my part to help my fellow believers be transformed into the image of Christ."

I am privileged to be working in a congregation where many have adopted this mind-set and are serving joyfully in ways that free me to joyfully use my gifts to do His good, pleasing and perfect will. On the Wednesday evening of the very week that I was developing the material for this chapter, I was walking across the parking lot to chair a meeting when I noticed a group of five or six people joyfully working to landscape the front of our church. They stayed at it till almost nine o'clock in the evening.

And because they were doing what they were gifted by God to do, the work was excellent and brought glory to God by beautifying the building associated with His name. That freed me to work equally competently in chairing my meeting. Each freed the other to do their work joyfully and for the good of the whole church. I also discovered that all their gardening supplies cost the church nothing because somebody else in the church had used their spiritual gift of giving to donate the plants and the topsoil, etc.

A second example was also brought to my attention the same week. Several times that week I walked past the temporary office of four young men and women who conduct our summer day camp—an outreach to our community. Their ministry involves very hard work for several weeks during which they are living sacrifices in more ways than one. They gave up the possibility of far more lucrative summer jobs in order to invest in the lives of children in the church and community.

Yet, as I walked past their office, more often than not I would hear singing coming from that room! They were singing while they worked—evidently experiencing their service as good, pleasing and perfect. And being just as ill-equipped to minister to children as I am at gardening, I, their pastor, rejoiced. They had freed me to study and preach, something they were not called or equipped to do.

Taking the Nature of a Servant

The texts we have explored so far in the context of this discipline of service have dealt almost exclusively with the gifts God has given us with which we can bless the body of Christ. We each have unique giftings, and if each of us serves the body through these appropriate gifts rather than delving into areas where we are not gifted, each of us is likely to be more effective and the body to be blessed. This also keeps us humble because when we serve in the area of our spiritual gifts, we cannot take any credit for the outcome because it is the result of a gracious gift from God. Thus, He gets the glory—spiritual worship again.

But the spiritual discipline of service extends beyond using our unique gifts. In fact, I am learning (very slowly) that the way we truly mature in this discipline of service is when we begin to serve in ways that diverge from where we are most gifted—where we humble ourselves and embrace the task of being a servant in the most basic sense.

There is a key Scripture in Philippians in which Paul speaks to this very issue:

> Your attitude should be the same as that of Christ Jesus:
> Who, being in very nature God,
> > did not consider equality with God something to
> > > be grasped,
> but made himself nothing,
> > taking the very nature of a servant,
> > being made in human likeness.
> And being found in appearance as a man,
> > he humbled himself
> > and became obedient to death—
> > > even death on a cross!
> Therefore God exalted him to the highest place
> > and gave him the name that is above every name,
> that at the name of Jesus every knee should bow,
> > in heaven and on earth and under the earth,
> and every tongue confess that Jesus Christ is Lord,
> > to the glory of God the Father. (2:5–11)

This phrase "being in very nature" comes from the Greek word *morphe,* a word that refers not just to external form but internal essence that expresses itself in a corresponding outward form.

In Greek mythology, there is a story of two of the Greek gods, Hermes and Zeus, who came down to earth disguised as slaves to find out how much homage humans were giving them. But once they found out what they wanted to know, they threw off their disguises and revealed themselves in all their Olympian splendor.

You see, they only took on an external form of humanity, while Jesus, in His incarnation, took on the real inner essence of humanity, and a servant at that. His outward appearance, as well as His acts of service and sacrifice, came from an actual inner essence of servanthood. He who was God became man, taking the form of a servant both inwardly and outwardly. In this way, He humbled Himself and served.

And if we are to be fully conformed to the image of Jesus Christ, we need to increasingly take on the *morphe* of a servant and not just its outward expression.

Ministry of the Mundane

In his book *The Life You've Always Wanted,* John Ortberg speaks to this ministry of servanthood, calling it the "ministry of the mundane," and there are countless opportunities that life offers us to play out this ministry every day of our lives. Perhaps there is a colleague at work who needs help in some way. Maybe a neighbor could use some assistance with yard work, or is going through a rough time in his or her personal life and needs someone who cares. Or how about that person with the flat tire by the side of the road? To be honest, you would really rather ignore these needs, but you know you should help. Each of these, and an unlimited number of others you come across every day, are all in the category of the ministry of the mundane—or as Ortberg also refers to it, the ministry of availability.[2]

These are settings in which the spiritual discipline of service has nothing to do with giftedness but is simply about being present and available. Ortberg observes that God never exempts anyone from the mundane, because it is a vital part of His character development curriculum: "Nobody is too good to perform the lowliest task.

People who worry about the loss of time that such petty, outward acts of helpfulness might entail are probably taking themselves and their careers too seriously." [3]

Much of this ministry of the mundane is carried out behind the scenes where no one will ever see what you are doing. It is the "secret service" aspect of this ministry that makes it so powerful in helping to mold your character into the image of Christ. It is also what makes it one of the least popular ministries to which the Lord calls His people. After all, there is nothing exhilarating about washing the dishes, changing a diaper, mowing someone's lawn, visiting a lonely shut-in—or any other service where no spotlight is shining and no kudos offered.

Richard Foster notes,

> More than any other single way, the grace of humility is worked into our lives through the Discipline of service. . . . Nothing *disciplines* the inordinate desires of the flesh like service, and nothing transforms the desires of the flesh like serving in hiddenness. The flesh whines against service but screams against hidden service. It strains and pulls for honor and recognition.[4]

Finding the Balance

Of course, each of us must find the right balance between the service we render to the body of Christ through our gifts and the service we provide through merely being available. The great eighteenth-century theologian and preacher Jonathan Edwards concluded that he would not be of much value to his congregation through visiting them in their homes. He was of far more value to the body of Christ as a preacher, and so he would spend most of his time (thirteen hours a day, according to some biographers) studying and preparing sermons. History confirms that this was a wise choice, as we look back on the dramatic spiritual revivals that happened throughout colonial America because of his ministry—and as we witness the impact his writings continue to have on the church some 350 years later.

In sharp contrast is a seventeenth-century puritan pastor named Richard Baxter who ministered for nearly twenty years in the English town of Kidderminster. Baxter was a dedicated pastor and not a theologian; his goal was to regularly visit the homes of his parishioners. His parish visits went much further than a simple cup of tea and light conversation polished off by a prayer of blessing.

When Baxter visited a home, he would assemble the entire family from the head of the house on down, including all the servants. Then he would proceed to teach both young and old the crucial tenets of their Christian faith. He would also make sure that the head of the house was teaching his wife, children and servants. Baxter took this part of his pastoral responsibilities very seriously, and after fourteen years the entire town of Kidderminster had experienced a deep spiritual transformation.

Here were two individuals with two completely different, but profoundly important, gifts for the body of Christ. Because each focused his giftings appropriately and did not attempt to do something God had not gifted him to do, whole communities and nations were transformed. So the question becomes: When should the ministry of the mundane be allowed to interrupt the focus of your unique spiritual gifts? I have found these different, yet complementary, observations by three different individuals helpful in thinking through this question.

John Ortberg suggests this wise rule of thumb: "Generally speaking, the higher our grandiosity quotient, the greater our need for this ministry."[5] In other words, the more we tend to think we are too important—or too busy—to stoop to the ministry of the mundane, the more we probably need it in our lives.

In *The Spirit of the Disciplines: Understanding How God Changes Lives,* Dallas Willard writes that "the discipline of service is even more important for Christians who find themselves in positions of influence, power, and leadership. To live as a servant while fulfilling socially important roles is one of the greatest challenges any disciple ever faces." He goes on to explain that those who would be great in God's kingdom can attain that greatness only "through the discipline of service in the power of God, for that alone will train them to exercise great power without corrupting their souls."[6]

If your calling is to some highly visible or otherwise important position that tends to isolate you from this ministry of the mundane, you might want to intentionally place yourself directly in the path of someone with a need that can only be met down in the trenches, below the radar screen of public esteem.

Rick Warren also addresses this question by noting that our primary ministry is through our spiritual gifts; and our secondary ministry is wherever you are needed at the moment.[7] Let's say I'm on the way to the church library to spend some time researching my sermon (my primary ministry). As I am opening the library door, I see someone outside the main entrance to the church, weighed down with several packages. I am needed. So I must recognize and allow my secondary ministry to interrupt my primary ministry, open the door and help that person carry the packages in.

And just in case Ortberg, Willard and Warren are not enough to convince us, Scripture has the last word to clinch the matter. The Apostle Paul puts it this way: "If you think you are too important to help someone, you are only fooling yourself. You are not that important" (Galatians 6:3, NLT).

"Go and Do Likewise"

One of the most powerful biblical illustrations of street-level servanthood is the well-known story of the Good Samaritan, told by Christ in Luke 10. Asked by an expert in the law what one must do to inherit eternal life, Jesus answered by having this lawyer quote the Old Testament passage that we have embraced within the pages of this book as crucial to catching the wind of the Spirit: "'Love the Lord your God with all your heart and with all your soul and with all your strength and with all your mind'; and, 'Love your neighbor as yourself'" (10:27).

"And who is my neighbor?" asked the lawyer (10:29).

That question prompted Jesus to tell a parable that goes to the very core of our duty as Christ-followers to respond to the needs of those around us with the heart of a servant. Most of us know the story well: A man on a journey is attacked by thieves, beaten and left for dead along the side of the road; as he lies bleeding and broken, three men pass by, all with the wherewithal to help him out. The first two are high-level Jewish religious leaders, both most certainly equipped with a knowledge of Scripture and each with a narrowly defined "ministry gift" in which they no doubt operate to the letter of the law. Both of these esteemed and respected spiritual leaders see the need of this broken man—and intentionally avoid him so they don't have to get involved.

The third man to come along has no defined ministry gifting. In fact he is nothing more than a lowly Samaritan, a people group despised by the Jews. Moved with compassion by the desperate need of the beaten and broken man by the side of the road, this humble Samaritan embraces the ministry of the mundane, giving both of himself and of his resources to someone he does not even know.

As Jesus concluded this pointed parable on the importance of loving and serving those around us—both within and outside the household of faith—He put an exclamation point on the whole thing with four simple words that give us our marching orders for serving as committed Christ-followers: "Go and do likewise" (Luke 10:37).

He who commissions us to serve also liberates us to do so. The shape of the various chapters in this book came largely from a series of messages I preached in our own church. These Sunday morning messages were complemented by a group Bible study on the fruit of the Spirit undertaken by nearly 250 people from our congregation. In the introductory video to this series, "Living Beyond Yourself," the author drew our attention to the familiar story of Jesus at the tomb of Lazarus. He had been dead and buried for four days. After ordering the people to roll away the burial stone, Jesus said, "Lazarus, come out!" The once-dead Lazarus, staggered out, almost tripping over his grave clothes. (See John 11:38–44.)

The author then invited us to substitute our name for Lazarus in Jesus' liberating command to come forth. The call to pursue the spiritual discipline of service is nothing less than a call to break out of the bondage to self that is keeping us from discovering the good, pleasing and perfect will of God in serving one another.

It is my prayer, for myself and for you, that this chapter will serve as an expanded version of Jesus' command and call to serve. May He who commissions us to "Go and do likewise" also call you by name, saying, "Come forth!"

Questions for Group Study

1. The opening quote in this chapter emphasizes our need for "the inner life of devotion, the outer life of service, and the intellectual life of rationality." Which of these are you weakest in? Has this book and group study made a difference in these areas?

2. Read Romans 12:1–8. What does it mean to be a "living sacrifice"? How does this affect the attitude we need to have toward the exercise of our spiritual gifts?

3. Read Ephesians 4:11–13. What is the role of "apostles, prophets, evangelists, pastors and teachers"? Who is performing the "works of service"? Discuss what some of these "works of service" might be.

4. How is the "ministry of the mundane" different from exercising our spiritual gifts? What does service based on availability, rather than gifting, teach us?

5. Spend some time in prayer, asking the Lord to show you specific ways that you can fulfill His command to "go and do likewise" and His call to "come forth" and serve.

Chapter 9

A Journey in Outrageous Giving

by Dale Losch

On June 5, 1982, I made two decisions that would radically affect the course of my life. While the actual decisions were made earlier, this was the date on which both were sealed, when I walked the aisle with my bride-to-be. Though I could talk for hours about the positive impact of our decision to become husband and wife that day, it is the other decision we made that I'd like to speak about.

It actually began about five months prior to our wedding, when my wife-to-be called to say that she had heard a message on the stewardship of our resources and she thought we should talk about the topic. As a result of that message, and our discussion, came an important decision that we would make our wedding anniversary not just a celebration of our union, but an opportunity to evaluate our giving during the previous year—and with God's help to raise our sights a little higher in the year ahead.

It was for us the beginning of what I call a "Journey in Outrageous Giving." For the entirety of our married life, twenty-eight years at this writing, we've been doing just that—giving outrageously—and I can honestly say it has been one of the most exciting journeys of our lives.

Outside the Box

I have chosen the word "outrageous" to communicate two very different facets of giving. The word communicates the idea of that which is shocking, unthinkable, offensive or outside accepted bounds. Biblical giving is all of the above. The idea of giving significant amounts of one's personal resources back to God has shocked and offended people from the very beginning of time, right down to the present day.

Do you realize that the first homicide in human history was committed because a man by the name of Cain was shocked and offended by God's expectations of his giving? He killed his brother Abel because God was pleased with Abel's giving, but was not pleased with his own (see Genesis 4). Not only does the Old Testament open with a conflict concerning giving, but it also ends with one. In Malachi, the last book of the Old Testament, God calls the people of Israel to task for depriving Him of the 10 percent He expected them to give as part of their worship.

Just as humanity's early history was marred by a giving-related death, so were the earliest days of the church, when Ananias and his wife, Sapphira, were struck dead after being exposed in a deception about what they had given to God (see Acts 5).

And how about the reactions that individuals in Jesus' day had to His teaching on giving? Jesus actually had more to say about money and giving than just about any other topic He addressed, and many found His teaching on the subject so offensive that they stopped following Him. Others simply stood by and ridiculed Him. In the Gospel of Luke—in which one in six verses has something to say about money and possessions—Jesus tells a parable about money and stewardship, which He concludes with the warning: "No servant can serve two masters. Either he will hate the one and love the other, or he will be devoted to the one and despise the other. You cannot serve both God and Money" (16:13). To which the Pharisees, "who loved money," responded by "sneering at Jesus" (16:14).

Biblical giving always has been, and always will be, outrageous—in a wonderfully positive sense! When properly understood and embraced, giving as God commands becomes a shockingly, unthinkably, wonderfully "outside-of-the-box" experience that you will never get tired of.

Embracing the Privilege

I find it strange that anyone could be negatively impacted by what God has to say about money and giving. In reality, giving God's way is such a powerfully positive experience that as Christians we should thank Him every day for the privilege of being givers into His kingdom. For example, consider Jesus' astounding declaration, "It is more blessed to give than to receive" (Acts 20:35). If, as His followers, we take Christ's words at face value, this simple statement represents an invitation into one of the greatest pleasures available to us!

If you're anything like me, you enjoy being on the receiving end of things. One of my favorite times of the year is tax time, not because I look forward to the paperwork involved in filling out my return, but because I know that I will receive a nice refund from the government. I also enjoy receiving a wide variety of other good things like compliments on a job well done, backrubs from my children, home-cooked meals from my wife, front-row seats at a hockey game, and first place in anything that remotely involves competition. Let's not kid ourselves: Receiving is fantastic! But here is Jesus telling us, in effect, "If you think receiving is fun, just wait till you get the hang of giving!"

So if Jesus tells us giving is better than receiving, why aren't more people queuing up in the giving line? If God's Word really is the ultimate truth for us, shouldn't we all be giving every last penny we can scrape together so that we can get in on this blessing Jesus promises us?

It's a Discipline

The truth of the matter is that while biblical giving is, indeed, the portal to a whole host of blessings, it is at its core a spiritual discipline, just like all the other disciplines we have spent time studying in this book. And like any other spiritual discipline we cultivate in our lives, biblical giving takes … well … discipline! If I want to cultivate the discipline of prayer in my spiritual life, I am going to have to work at it. Reading the Bible through on a regular basis, becoming a real student of Scripture, or embracing the discipline of godly service—

all of these disciplines are going to involve effort, training and discipline on my part. Likewise, godly, outrageous giving will only come through discipline.

With the abundant promises about money and giving that fill God's Word, you might think it would be easy to give a significant portion of your income to God. But it can be excruciatingly difficult to dive into this discipline of giving. Expanding one's giving muscles into unthinkably outrageous realms is a work of faith that takes time. So how do you get there? How do you catch the wind of the Spirit and soar into new realms in this spiritual discipline of giving?

It's an Act of Faith

Anyone who ever attended Sunday school as a child is familiar with the name Zacchaeus. His is one of those stories that, along with the one about David and Goliath, always seems to make it into the curriculum. What is interesting, however, is that Zacchaeus is best known for the size of his stature rather than for what was truly amazing about him—the size of his faith.

Zacchaeus' story, recorded in the Gospel of Luke, is fascinating on a number of levels, the first of which is its description of the man. The first few verses of Luke 19 offer three interesting details about Zacchaeus: one, he was the chief tax collector; two, he was wealthy; and three, he was unusually short.

As a tax collector, he would have been considered a marked man in Jewish society, considered a traitor for collaborating with the enemy and a cheat for gouging people for more taxes than they owed. Because he was the chief tax collector, it is reasonable to assume that he was more corrupt than average. In all likelihood, Zacchaeus was one of the most despised men in town.

Luke also chooses to mention that Zacchaeus was wealthy, one of two men of means mentioned by Luke in as many chapters. The other man, recorded in Luke 18:18, was a rich Jewish ruler who asked Jesus what he had to do to get to heaven. It is obvious that Luke wanted his readers to note the contrast between these two wealthy individuals. One was a Jewish ruler; the other, a Jewish traitor. One was respected, the other despised. One followed the law of God, while the other collaborated with the laws of Rome. One was the cream of the crop, the other the "scum of the earth."

Finally, Luke mentions that Zacchaeus was "a short man," or as the King James Version puts it, he was "little of stature." Simply put, Zacchaeus was a pip-squeak, which makes it quite certain that in every way, those around him looked down on Zacchaeus as despised and inferior. But Jesus didn't.

The story is not only fascinating in its description of the man but in its description of Zacchaeus' encounter with Jesus. It is noteworthy that while others despised this little man, Jesus knew him by name and was not ashamed to acknowledge him. The same is true today when it comes to each one of us. No matter who we are, where we have been or what we have done, the Lord Jesus knows us and reaches out to us in love. Furthermore, we read that Zacchaeus "welcomed him gladly" (19:6). This is in contrast to the rich man in the previous chapter, who sadly departed from Christ (18:23), and in contrast to the crowds who grumbled about Jesus' choice of associates.

Finally, the story is fascinating in its description of the outcome of the encounter between Christ and Zacchaeus. Though very little detail is given as to what led up to it, the response of Zacchaeus to Jesus' intervention in his life focuses on money. And Jesus responded by indicating that Zacchaeus demonstrated saving faith, declaring, "Today salvation has come to this house, because this man, too, is a son of Abraham" (Luke 19:9).

By calling Zacchaeus a "son of Abraham," Jesus was saying the same thing that Paul would declare years later when he explains that only those who believe are truly "children of Abraham" (Galatians 3:7). In other words, Jesus was saying in effect, "Zacchaeus has experienced salvation today, because he has expressed his faith in Me."

An Amazing Declaration

But what led Jesus to this conclusion about Zacchaeus? Besides the fact that Jesus knows the hearts of men and could discern that this man's faith was genuine, Luke mentions only one detail that apparently demonstrated the genuine transformation of this despised little man. It had to do with his money. Zacchaeus made this astounding declaration: "Here and now I give half of my possessions to the poor, and if I have cheated anybody out of anything, I will pay back four times the amount" (Luke 19:8).

To understand the implications of what he said, let's suppose that Zacchaeus had a net worth of $1 million in today's currency. What happened to all his money once he came to faith in Jesus? First of all, Zacchaeus made a commitment to give away half of it to the poor. Where on earth did he get that idea? Either Jesus talked to him about it or somehow he just knew that investing his resources in this way was the right thing to do.

But Zacchaeus wasn't finished. He went on to say that if he had defrauded anyone of anything, he would pay it back—not dollar for dollar, but four to one! This was in keeping with the Old Testament standard of restitution. We don't know how much of Zacchaeus' wealth was obtained by underhanded means, but it would not be at all unreasonable to suggest that 10 percent came through fraud. This would translate to $100,000 of his total net worth. If he were to repay those he cheated with a four-to-one ratio, that would amount to another payout of $400,000, leaving him with only one-tenth of his original wealth. In reality, Zacchaeus didn't give a tithe—he kept a tithe. What an incredible act of faith!

Start at the Beginning

Outrageous biblical giving begins as an act of faith. Earlier we mentioned the story of Cain and Abel. Here is what the writer of Hebrews says about Abel's giving: "By faith Abel offered God a better sacrifice than Cain did. By faith he was commended as a righteous man, when God spoke well of his offerings" (Hebrews 11:4). Giving to God the first and the best of what you have— when you could legitimately use it to your own benefit —is an act of faith.

I have always been of the conviction that the starting point of biblical giving is 10 percent, what has been traditionally called a "tithe." From childhood I was taught to give at least a tenth of my gross income to God, and I have taught my children the same. When one starts applying this truth at a young age with such income as an allowance or babysitting money, it is not a difficult discipline to follow through with into adulthood. Nonetheless, it can sometimes become a great challenge when one's income begins to increase.

I remember the day our oldest son was deeply impacted in the matter of giving as an act of faith. In the summer between his freshman and sophomore years of university, Joel landed his first high-paying job, working the night shift loading trucks for a local food distributor where every dollar he earned was well deserved. When he brought home his first two-week paycheck, he was shocked to discover that the government had taken 20 percent of his hard-earned money in taxes! Suddenly his $1,100 paycheck had shrunk to $880. My words of "welcome to the working world" were of small comfort to his tortured soul.

But he knew he wasn't finished. Not only did he still want to give God at least a tenth, but he was faced with the age-old question, "Do I tithe on the gross amount, or on the net?" Convinced that because God had given him the gross he should give back to God accordingly, Joel wrote out a check for $110, meaning that his original $1,100 had now been reduced to about $770. Admittedly, it is discouraging for a college student who faces thousands of dollars in tuition fees to watch his first paycheck evaporate like drops of water on a hot grill. Nonetheless he went ahead and did it.

The following Sunday after the church service, our family stopped at our church mail slot and pulled out an assortment of prayer letters and announcements along with an envelope addressed to Joel. Shortly after getting home, I walked past his room and noticed him sitting on his bed obviously lost in thought. I decided to go in and ask him what he was thinking about. Almost immediately tears of joy filled his eyes.

"God is just so good to me," he said. "Last week when I wrote my check to the church, it was really hard because I felt like I needed that money for school. Then He gives me this," he said, indicating the envelope bearing his name. He removed a check, written from a family friend who had moved away a year earlier and had sent a little something to help with Joel's college costs. The check was for $150. "It's just like you told me, Dad," he said, smiling through his tears. "You can't out-give God."

Yes, biblical giving begins as an act of faith. To choose to give God 10 percent—or more—of what you may legitimately need is outrageous, shocking, and unthinkable. But if you wait until you think you can afford it, you'll never do it. You simply have to take that step of faith and give.

An Advance of Faith

In 2 Corinthians 8:7, the Apostle Paul writes: "But just as you excel in everything—in faith, in speech, in knowledge, in complete earnestness and in your love for us—see that you also excel in this grace of giving."

Back in 1982, it was this foundational verse that really launched my wife and me on the journey of outrageous giving. Paul is urging the believers at Corinth to aggressively advance in their capacity to give to the needs of others, following the example of the believers in Macedonia, who in spite of their deep poverty not only "gave as much as they were able, and even beyond their ability," but "urgently pleaded with us for the privilege of sharing in this service to the saints."

As a result of this passage, every year on our anniversary we have asked ourselves two questions: First, "Has God been faithful to meet all our needs this past year when we gave 'x' percent of our income?" Without fail, the answer to this question during the entirety of our marriage has been a resounding "Yes!"

Second, we have asked ourselves, "Can we trust Him to increase our giving by 'x' percent this year?" While the percentage of increase has varied from year to year, sometimes a whole number and others only a fraction, rarely have we remained static in our giving. This has been one of the most exciting, liberating advances of faith we have ever known. Has it been stretching? Yes! Has it been difficult? Yes, profoundly at times. Has it weakened, handicapped or grounded us? The answer is a resounding "No!" Rather, it has allowed us to soar!

Moving Past the "Training Wheels"

Here is an illustration. When our first child was three years old, we bought him his first bicycle, a bright red one complete with horn, plastic basket on the handlebars and adjustable training wheels. The training wheels allowed him to ride the bike without tipping over. As he slowly developed his riding skills, we would raise the training wheels a notch at a time, so that he could learn to balance the bike without the aid of the extra wheels. The day finally came when he began to see the training wheels as restrictive. Rather than helping his progress, they seemed to slow him down. He wanted them removed. It was a triumphant day when he rode his little bike down the paved driveway in front of the house, free of the extra wheels that had formerly kept him upright.

But what did it mean to be "free"? Obviously he was now "free" to fall, but that was certainly not the desired goal. His freedom from the guiding influence of the training wheels was really a liberating freedom that allowed him to do far more than he had been able to do prior to their removal. He could now ride faster and maneuver more freely, leaning into corners and turning without the obstruction of those little wheels that had previously held him in a rigid upright position.

The regulating influence of the Old Testament laws concerning tithing—along with a host of other behaviors—acted in much the same way as those training wheels. Paul likened them to a tutor or schoolmaster who guides a child's progress until he reaches maturity. The removal of the training wheels does not eliminate our need to live according to the principles learned while under their influence. Rather, it enhances our ability not only to live by them, but to surpass them. It opens us up to new avenues of faith.

An Adventure of Faith

The journey in the spiritual discipline of giving has been one of the most rewarding adventures of our lives. My wife and I do not tell people what we give because that is for us a very intimate part of our relationship with God. But I will say that as we have stepped out in faith over the past many years in this discipline of giving, our "faith muscles" have grown dramatically. Far more amazing, however, than what God has enabled us to give is what He has given in return. I am reminded of story after story of God's abundance to us, some of them so amazing that I would almost be embarrassed to share them. It has been an incredible adventure that is best described by the words of Paul:

> Remember this: Whoever sows sparingly will also reap sparingly, and whoever sows generously will also reap generously. Each man should give what he has decided in his heart to give, not reluctantly or under compulsion, for God loves a cheerful giver. And God is able to make all grace abound to you, so that in all things at all times, having all that you need, you will abound in every good work. (2 Corinthians 9:6–8)

The process of sowing and reaping is nothing short of miraculous. If a farmer sows a bushel of seed, he'll reap a truck full. If he sows a truck full, he'll reap a barn full. If he sows a barn full, he'll reap a train full. But if he stops sowing and instead consumes his seed, then he'll stop reaping.

The same goes for the spiritual principle of biblical giving. I cannot explain it, but I'm living it. The more we give, the more He seems to keep pouring back on us—not so that we can keep it all, but so that we can give even more. I honestly feel like a man who has discovered the greatest investment strategy of all time and wonders why so few others are in the know.

Do It Hilariously

Do you want to see God pour out His abundance in your life? Then you must grow in your generosity—not so you can keep it all but so that you can keep giving even more generously. I'm not telling you *what* you should give. God will tell you that. As Paul exhorts, each of us "should give what he has decided in his heart to give."

But I assure you that God wants you to grow, He wants you TO flex your faith muscles—He wants you to pull off those training wheels and experience the liberty of the Spirit of God in your giving. Why? Because God loves a "cheerful giver." The Greek word for "cheerful" is *hilaros*, from which we get our English word "hilarious." In the world of humor, hilarious is not merely something that makes you smile. It is not even something that makes you laugh. It is something that makes you laugh so hard you cry. It is not forced. It is not fabricated. It is not done in measured, controlled installments. Rather, it is something so funny that it bursts forth in unrestrained fits of laughter that hurt your stomach and cause your eyes to overflow with tears.

Imagine giving to God in that same way, in a manner that is not forced or fabricated, not measured or programmed, but pure, unrestrained, joy-driven and right from the heart. That's the kind of giving God longs to see bursting forth from His people. You cannot put a percentage value on it, because it has little to do with percentages and everything to do with passion.

Embracing "hilarious" giving begins as an act of faith, it grows as an advance of faith and it becomes a lifelong adventure of faith. Let me urge you to spread your wings of faith and catch an updraft of the Spirit of God who alone can cause you to soar to new heights in this incredible spiritual journey.

Questions for Group Study

1. "Shocking, unthinkable, offensive or outside accepted bounds" are all words that could define the word "outrageous." In what ways might Jesus' teaching on money fit that definition?

2. Are there aspects of our modern Western culture that make Jesus' teaching on money and giving seem all the more "outrageous"? What specific ways can we live that can serve as a balance to this cultural influence?

3. Read Luke 19:1–10. What is the connection between Zacchaeus' statement in verse 8 and Jesus' declaration in verse 9? How is one's use of his resources an expression of faith?

4. Read 2 Corinthians 8:1–7. What did Paul mean by his exhortation to "excel in this grace of giving"? In what ways have you grown in the grace of giving in the past year? What are some ways that one could stretch himself/ herself further in the stewardship of his/her resources?

5. Read 2 Corinthians 9:6–11. If generosity with the resources God has entrusted to us truly does work on the same principle as sowing and reaping, why do you think more people don't embark on such an adventure? How has your own journey in generosity been a great adventure? How have you seen God respond to your faith in giving?

Chapter 10

Imagination

Over the last several chapters we have been exploring the dimensions of eight spiritual disciplines, sails that we must learn to hoist if we are to catch the wind of the Spirit and be gradually and progressively transformed into the image of Christ. We have taken a close look at worship, Scripture reading and meditation, study, prayer, confession, fellowship, service and giving. We also learned that the whole process begins by genuine conversion—one mark of which is the birth and permanent presence of a desire to become like Christ our Savior and Lord.

We have been getting a grasp on these spiritual disciplines by and large through the avenue of explanation, learning the parameters of each discipline and how they are intended to function in our lives. Explanation is a vital process in learning, but there is another equally

vital process that works in tandem with explanation
and is crucial to internalizing each of these disciplines
and making them a reality in our lives. That process is
imagination.

Author Eugene Peterson writes eloquently and with
great insight about the synergy between these two pro-
cesses.

> Explanation pins things down so that we can handle
> and use them—obey and teach, help and guide.
> Imagination opens things up so that we can grow into
> maturity—worship and adore, exclaim and honor,
> follow and trust. Explanation restricts and defines
> and holds down; imagination expands and lets loose.
> Explanation keeps our feet on the ground; imagination
> lifts our heads into the clouds. Explanation puts us in
> harness; imagination catapults us into mystery.[1]

In this closing chapter, I want to harness the power
of imagination, broadly understood, to help consolidate
the practice of the spiritual disciplines for the rest of our
lives. Specifically, I want to leave you with one or more
images for each of the eight spiritual disciplines that we
have studied so far. (By "image" I'm referring not only to
obvious entities like photographs or statues, but also to
stories, poetry, metaphors and the like.)

Moreover, I have tried to choose those images that
have actually worked in combination with explanation
to motivate me in the practice of these spiritual disciplines, although some have worked more powerfully
than others. I'm aware that the images that have gripped
me most powerfully might not "work" for you, so my
goal here is not to harness you to my images, but to help
you understand how imagination works together with

explanation to bring imaginative momentum in my own life for each of these disciplines. My prayer is that God will give you your own unique images that are consistent with your unique personality, background and emotional makeup.

Conversion

Before we tackle the images for the individual spiritual disciplines, I want to take a few moments to address the image for conversion itself. In chapter 1 we learned that conversion is nothing less than an encounter with Jesus Christ that changes our understanding of who He is and who we are, and results in our leaving our past behind and following Him for the rest of our lives.

Often non-Christians will attempt to draw a comparison between the good lifestyle of a non-Christian and the questionable lifestyles of some people they know who claim to be Christians, and conclude that there is really nothing substantive at the core of the Christian faith. "After all," they will argue, "this individual with no faith in Christ is living a far more upright and gracious lifestyle than most Christians we know."

The fundamental flaw with this argument, as C.S. Lewis has pointed out, is that it does not recognize that the non-Christian's "niceness" is not his gift to God but God's gift to him (a specific instance of what theologians call common grace). So the proper question to ask, the real measure for conversion, is not how a particular Christian stacks up against a reasonably well-behaved non-Christian, but how and to what degree each of those lives would have been affected, in one case by Christ's presence and in the other by His absence.

A dramatic example of this, one I have thought a lot about over the years, is the conversion of my father-in-law. (I have my wife's permission to share this story.) For much of his life, he was a nominal Christian from an Anglican background. He worked hard to provide for his family, was considered by those who knew him to be a good man, but he really didn't have any meaningful relationship with Christ at all.

But when he finally became a committed Christ-follower, every part of his life was impacted by his faith. One of the most dramatic changes happened in an area with which he had struggled for most of his life—outbursts of anger, which would often be unleashed upon those who were the closest to him.

After my father-in-law became a true believer, I had the privilege of serving with him on the elders board of the church we both attended. One Saturday evening he called me on the phone with a spiritual dilemma. As an elder, he was scheduled the next day to serve Communion to the congregation, but he was deeply convicted about a relational conflict with a family member. "I feel guilty serving Communion with this conflict hanging over me," he confided to me. "What do you think I should do?"

"Are you asking me as your son-in-law, or are you asking me as a fellow Christian?" I asked him.

"As a fellow Christian," he responded.

"In that case, I really think you need to forget that you are decades older than this individual. You need to pick up the phone, call him and apologize for whatever part you played in this breach in your relationship."

I am pleased to tell you that he did just what I had counseled, and there was a magnificent reconciliation with the individual involved. But my real point in telling this story is to point out that before my father-in-law committed his life to Christ, such a response would have been inconceivable. That one incident will always serve as a powerful image in my life to work alongside the various intellectual explanations of conversion.

Worship

In chapter 2 we learned that we become like the One we worship; we are touched and transformed by an encounter with His greatness. In order to give you a sustaining image for this spiritual discipline of transforming worship of God, I want to walk you through how we respond to greatness or hugeness at the physical level, because how we respond in that realm can actually mirror the very different ways in which God has created us to respond to greatness that we encounter in worship. (Before reading any further, pause for a few moments and recall an actual specific encounter with creation's hugeness—be it standing on the edge of the Grand Canyon, beholding the Swiss Alps or contemplating the vastness of the Milky Way. This might help you personalize the discussion that follows.)

In his book *Forging a Real World Faith,* Gordon MacDonald notes that he has observed six distinctive leading instincts that govern the worship of Christians. He notes further that each of these instincts has a particular agenda associated with it. He concludes by observing that these instincts influence the unique manner in which each of us responds to God in worship.

The first of these is the aesthetic instinct. For individuals dominated by the aesthetic instinct, majesty is the dominant agenda. Individuals with this instinct will want to capture the greatness on camera or paint it. When it comes to worship, they'll want the biggest wide-angle lens available for their spiritual camera, the largest spiritual canvas on which to interpret God's grandeur. This is what they hope to "get" in worship. Disregard for God's majesty by those who lead in worship gets in their way and bothers them to no end.

The second leading instinct guiding individuals in their worship is the experiential instinct, with joy as the accompanying agenda. Individuals influenced by this instinct respond to a beautiful mountain with hiking boots rather than a camera or paintbrush. They want to touch the mountain, feel the rocks under their feet and struggle with its inclines and geography until they reach its summit. In worship, these are the people who rise or clap their hands, and perhaps even dance a little. King David, celebrating before the ark with all his might is a perfect example.

A third group of worshipers are influenced by the activist instinct, and their agenda is achievement. These are the people who will go to the foot of the mountain and be furious to find that somebody has constructed a factory next to it that is belching smoke. They will organize groups that will march around the factory. They will write letters. They will try to get that factory shut down and removed. In the realm of worship these are the ones who feel God's presence when they are on the move. They will write letters to politicians on issues that touch upon their faith in the public square. They will organize marches to protest situations that represent a social wrong. This is how they honor God.

Then we have individuals who are motivated in worship by the contemplative instinct. Their agenda is listening. When these people go to the foot of the mountain, they don't really care about cameras, hiking boots or the nearby factory. As long as there is a quiet place in full sight of the mountain, they are content. In the worship service, these are people who say, "Can we please tone down the volume a bit? Can we not have at least a few moments of silence?" Doesn't the psalmist tell us to be still and know that He is God?

For those influenced by the student instinct, truth is the primary agenda. These are the people for whom a guidebook is essential before they take off for the mountain. They want to find out how the mountain was formed in the first place. In a worship setting these people cannot fully enter into a song unless they are satisfied as to the theological accuracy of the words. They get irritated by preachers who do not "stick to the Word." They usually take copious notes during the sermon and are not afraid to challenge what they perceive as erroneous teaching or departure from the Word of God.

Finally, there are those whose worship is governed by the relational instinct, and their agenda is love. These people will seldom if ever be found alone at the foot of the mountain because they want to share the beauty of the experience with others. In a worship setting, they come to church not only for the vertical connection with God but the horizontal connection with the people. They worship just as much, if not more, in the lobby before and after a service, than in the sanctuary.

That's how and why my response to bigness in creation has served as a sustaining image for my worship. Most of us have one or two of these leading instincts that motivate our worship, and our response to bigness in creation gives us a clue to that. So the next time you find yourself confronted with something grand in nature, check your response. It may be the voice of the Lord saying personally to you, "That's the way I want you to worship."

Scripture Reading and Meditation

In chapter 3 we discussed the importance of immersing ourselves regularly in Scripture through reading and meditation—not for the purpose of absorbing information, but to hear God speak to us. We have already looked at one image in relation to our interaction with God's Word, and that is the metaphor of the Bible as a five-act play into which God has written you and me as actors and actresses integral to the plot.

In Acts 1 and 2 we are introduced in quick succession to creation and the fall of mankind through the sin of Adam and Eve. In Act Three we witness God's call to Israel to become His chosen people to put the world right—and Israel's failure to effectively embrace this call. In Act Four Jesus Christ Himself appears—the one true Israelite who did what the nation was supposed to do but didn't—through whom God could accomplish His redemptive agenda. Act Five opens with Scene One, the penning of the New Testament, and in Scene Two you and I finally take the stage, with God the ultimate producer of this grand and historic drama giving us our cues from everything that has gone on before us in the history of Scripture.

While this in itself provides us with an adequate and sustaining metaphor, I want to offer a second image that I believe will help you embrace this discipline of Scripture reading and meditation. Twice in Scripture we have God's servants—Ezekiel and John—being told to "eat" God's word and then speak (Ezekiel 3:3–4; Revelation 10:9–11) and once Jeremiah exclaiming that he ate God's word with joy and delight (Jeremiah 15:16).

The image of "eating" God's Word has always been a powerful motivator for me. What we eat becomes part of us as the miraculous chemical factories inside our bodies break the food down, extract the nutrients and end up building tissues and organs and giving us the energy to live with gusto and enjoyment, glad to be alive. No wonder God's Word is described in various food metaphors—milk and meat, water and honey, grain, finest of wheat, etc.

This metaphor of eating the Word continually delivers me from lapsing into the error of reading Scripture to fulfill a legalistic regimen. It reminds me instead that as I read, I am nourishing the spiritual equivalent of tissues and organs essential for my soul's health and strength. Then, as I follow the example of Ezekiel, Jeremiah and John and preach it, I feed others with soul food. The five-act drama of redemption and "eat the book" are two images that work powerfully in tandem with my intellect when it comes to this spiritual discipline.

Study

In chapter 4 we explored the spiritual discipline of

renewing the mind through disciplined study. One story from the Old Testament has for me become an enduring metaphor for the discipline of study. King Josiah was one of the few godly kings in the history of Israel. He was only eight years old when he took the throne, and Scripture relates that "he did that which was right in the sight of the LORD, and walked in all the way of David his father, and turned not aside to the right hand or to the left" (2 Kings 22:2, KJV). One of the projects he took on as king was to renovate the temple which his father had allowed to fall into total disrepair.

During the time that the temple was being repaired, workers actually uncovered the "book of the law" (either Deuteronomy or the Pentateuch—Genesis to Deuteronomy). When King Josiah heard what was contained in this book of the law, he was appalled by how far his forefathers and his nation had drifted from these biblical moorings. In great fear of divine judgment for this serious violation of covenant responsibilities, Josiah inquired of the prophetess Huldah, who confirmed Josiah's worst fears regarding divine judgment. Josiah's response to this word was to humble himself before God and to launch a national movement of spiritual reform. He gathered the nation together and had them listen for several hours as the Word of God was read before them, followed by a solemn ceremony during which all the people covenanted together to follow God's law once more.

Now think about it: The contents of this book were a thousand years old, and yet it was still powerful enough to change the hearts and lives of an entire nation. Tell me, is there any other centuries-old book, the contents of which can bring such radical renewal in its domain of interest? What doctor, upon finding a book of medicine written a thousand years ago, would look at its contents with anything more than mild curiosity? What book on chemistry, biology, or astronomy of similar vintage would give us vital insights into those fields and launch a revolution today? Not one.

Several years ago I was out walking one morning, reading 2 Kings 22, when a new revelation struck me about this story. I had always had the impression that Josiah found the book, but as I contemplated this passage again, I felt as if God were saying to me, "No, Josiah didn't find the book; the book found him." With that realization, tears filled my eyes as God took me back to when I was seventeen years old, a two-week-old Christ-follower, and I found an old, tattered copy of a commentary on the book of Romans—a "find" that launched me on my primary calling to study and teach God's Word. Up until that morning, I had always said that "I found the book," but from that day on, I began to say that "the book found me."

That is why this story of Josiah has remained for me a powerful motivator for studying Scripture. I want to keep putting myself in a situation where the book can keep on finding me.

Prayer

In chapter 5 we considered the spiritual discipline of prayer, using Jesus' teaching on the Lord's Prayer as a framework. We learned that while we can pray about anything—our daily needs, our children, our job situations, our friends and neighbors—all our prayers must be subsumed under an overarching concern for the glory of God, captured in the petition "Your kingdom come, your will be done on earth as it is in heaven" (Matthew 6:10).

Several images and metaphors have helped me in my practice of such prayer, but space and time constrain me to share just one—a hymn that has helped me get into my prayer time on many occasions, especially when I have been stressed by internal or external chaos. There are some genres of literature that you can skim, but poetry is not one of them. So I invite you to slowly read the following verses of this beloved hymn written by the great American poet John Greenleaf Whittier:

> Dear Lord and Father of mankind,
> Forgive our foolish ways;
> Reclothe us in our rightful mind,
> In purer lives Thy service find,
> In deeper reverence, praise.
>
> In simple trust like theirs who heard,
> Beside the Syrian sea,
> The gracious calling of the Lord,
> Let us, like them, without a word,
> Rise up and follow Thee.
>
> O Sabbath rest by Galilee,
> O calm of hills above,
> Where Jesus knelt to share with Thee
> The silence of eternity,
> Interpreted by love!
>
> With that deep hush subduing all
> Our words and works that drown
> The tender whisper of Thy call,
> As noiseless let Thy blessing fall
> As fell Thy manna down.

Drop Thy still dews of quietness,
Till all our strivings cease;
Take from our souls the strain and stress,
And let our ordered lives confess
The beauty of Thy peace.

Breathe through the heats of our desire
Thy coolness and Thy balm;
Let sense be dumb, let flesh retire;
Speak through the earthquake, wind, and fire,
O still, small voice of calm.[2]

Read the words again, pausing to linger over the images that are conjured up by the words, and you will get a sense of how and why they function so effectively to get me in the right frame of mind to pray.

Confession

In chapter 6 we dealt with the crucial, but often overlooked, spiritual discipline of confession. We discussed the need for our confession to be radical—that we need to confess the fact of our sin, the depth of our sin and the defilement of our sin. We also discussed the need to cry out to God for radical renewal, to pray like King David prayed: "Create in me a pure heart, O God, and renew a steadfast spirit within me. Do not cast me from your presence or take your Holy Spirit from me. Restore to me the joy of your salvation and grant me a willing spirit, to sustain me" (Psalm 51:10–12).

One of the images that truly deserves the overwrought adjective "unforgettable" and that has sustained me with regards to this spiritual discipline is the story of Holocaust survivor Yehiel Dinur, who survived the horrors and hardships of the extermination camps supervised by Hitler henchman Adolph Eichmann. When Dinur entered the courtroom at Eichmann's Nuremberg trial and came face-to-face with his tormentor after so many years, he fell to the ground, his whole body wracked with sobbing.

Charles Colson writes that Mike Wallace interviewed Dinur and asked if the horrible memories of his time in the concentration camp had caused this reaction. Dinur said no. He explained that, back in the concentration camp, Eichmann had been a godlike figure to the inmates, holding their fate in his hands. He could keep them alive or have them killed in a number of excruciatingly painful ways. But in the courtroom, Dinur realized that Eichmann was an ordinary man, and that Dinur, under the right circumstances, could have committed the same atrocities Eichmann did. Dinur fell to the floor not because of painful memories, but because he realized that day that "I am capable to do this. *I am . . . exactly like he.*" Colson concludes, "Dinur, the Auschwitz survivor, is right—Eichmann is in us, each of us." [3]

Dinur's statement is truly chilling and epitomizes for me the need for continued, thoroughgoing, radical confession of the evil nature of our hearts before God. That's what will keep us aware of our desperate need for a Savior—and incredibly thankful that we have one.

Giving

In chapter 9 we learned about the joyous discipline of outrageous giving. We found that giving is an act of faith, an advance of faith and an adventure of faith.

Two images, one negative and one positive, have sustained me in this important discipline. In his essay "Notes on the Way," English author George Orwell recalls how a wasp landed on his plate one morning at breakfast and began sucking on the remnants of some jam. Orwell writes of how he took a knife, cut the wasp in half and then observed as the wasp, unaware of his fatal predicament, continued to suck on the jam even while it oozed out the other end of his severed body. It was only when it came time came for the wasp to fly away that it was forced to face its horrible fate.[4]

In a sense this severed wasp provides us with an image of the dreaded disease of consumerism that plagues our society. The more we have, the more we want; and many who have been ensnared by the unending assault of advertising that keeps telling us that we need more, bigger and better are totally unaware that they have become like that wasp, sucking it all in and losing it as fast as they acquire it—until the day comes for them to meet their Maker. Then it's too late.

Let's balance this powerful, though negative image, with an equally powerful positive one.

In the book of Malachi, we are told about a skeptical majority in Israel for whom the worship of Jehovah had become boring and this showed in their offerings of leftover, crippled, useless animals, while they saved their best for their human masters and for themselves. But a godly minority who feared God received this commendation from God: "But for you who revere my name, the sun of righteousness will rise with healing in its wings. And you will go out and leap like calves released from the stall" (Malachi 4:2).

I am not a farmer, so I am not certain how a calf reacts when it gets let out of a stall, but I can imagine. All of a sudden there are no boundaries, just exhilarating freedom, a sense of exuberance, joy and the anticipation of new arenas to be explored.

On one hand we have the image of a severed wasp and on the other a calf released from the stall—the bondage of consumerism and the freedom of glad worship through generous giving. The juxtaposition of these two images has served in my life as a powerful motivator to continue to practice the discipline of outrageous giving.

Service

"Hey, you skipped over a couple of the earlier disciplines," you might say. "What about images for service and fellowship?" Allow me to offer a couple of reasons for leaving these two for the last.

First of all, you will recall that in the spiritual discipline of service, one of the primary ways in which we perform this discipline is through the gifts God has given us. My primary gift is teaching the Word of God, and so the images for study and Scripture happen to be the same images that sustain me in my primary work of service. This might not be the case for you, so you need to discover sustaining images from the Scriptures, hymnology, the arts, stories and personal experience that will inspire and challenge you to serve the body of Christ through your gifts.

We also discussed how the discipline of service involves the ministry of the mundane—doing ordinary things under the radar for people in need. I'm only just beginning to grow in that area, and I do not have yet a powerful image that I can honestly share with you.

However, I can say that Foster's powerful indictment that our souls positively scream at the thought of secret service (calling up the image of my soul screaming for recognition even as I serve secretly) does motivate me to keep pursuing the ministry of the mundane.

Fellowship

In chapter 7 we learned about the discipline of fellowship, that it isn't primarily about coffee and cookies in the "fellowship hall." True fellowship comes out of a deep sense of oneness in Jesus to the extent that we find ourselves holding loosely to what is ours and saying to our fellow Christians, "What is mine is yours."

I find myself in a similar situation as I do with the discipline of secret service. These are not my strong points. For those who are like me, I suggest the story of Paul, Philemon and Onesimus. Paul sent the slave Onesimus back to his owner with instructions that Philemon must receive his errant slave back—not just as a slave but as a brother in Christ, just as Philemon would receive Paul himself. That story may serve as a starting point for a memorable image.

Discipline, Desire and Faith

The very week I concluded the series of messages that formed the basis for this book was also the start of Wimbledon, the world-famous tennis tournament. Roger Federer, probably the greatest player ever, was hoping to win his sixth Wimbledon in a row. Two young outstanding players stood in his way—Rafael Nadal and Novak Djokovich. Earlier that week, Djokovich was playing a Russian named Marat Safin. The commentators observed that Djokovich would probably win many more than Safin because he was much more disciplined, waking up each day asking himself, "How can I make myself a better player today than when I went to bed last night?" The commentators also pointed out that at the age of seven, Djokovich wanted to be number one in the world at this game.

The commentator had uncovered a crucial insight—that while discipline is essential for growth, it is not foundational. Underlying the discipline that characterized Djokovich's tennis life was the prior desire to be number one someday. There may have been many possible reasons for this desire—fame, fortune, the honor of his country, etc. We do not know and it does not matter for our purpose. Regardless of what motivated his desire to be the top tennis player, the common factor was the underlying belief that achieving his goal would bring him pleasure.

Underneath his discipline lay a desire, and underneath that desire lay a faith that if the desired object was achieved, it would bring joy. What is true of Djokovich in the world of tennis is true of all of us in all aspects of life, including our spiritual life. The spiritual disciplines we have studied in the preceding chapters, and for which I've given you sustaining images in this chapter, are essential. But we will only persevere in those disciplines if underlying them is the desire to be transformed into Christ's image. And we will desire that only if we believe that this journey of transformation into Christ's image will bring us lasting joy.

While this book addresses the understanding and practice of the spiritual disciplines, it can do very little, if anything, to produce either the desire to become like Jesus or the faith that such a transformation is the route to lasting joy. That is the work of the Spirit in your soul—a work for which you must desperately seek.

If you have developed no desire to become like Christ, however slowly and imperfectly, please reread the first chapter on conversion and cry out to God for such an encounter with Jesus as Peter had.

Questions for Group Study

1. What is the author's definition of "imagination" and "image"? Is an "image" useful to you to recall the various spiritual disciplines and remember their importance in your life? Why or why not?

2. Of the various images presented by the author, which ones do you find to be the most powerful and useful? Which ones do you find to be the least? The author encouraged his readers to come up with their own images if his do not work for them. Have any other images for the spiritual disciplines come to your mind?

3. The author mentions six "instincts" that govern how a person approaches worship: the aesthetic, the experiential, the activist, the contemplative, the student and the relational. Which of these categories do you fall into? Is it possible for a person to lean toward more than one of these instincts?

4. What is your overall reaction to the book? What concepts from the book made the biggest impact on you?

5. In which of the eight spiritual disciplines in the book (worship, Scripture, study, prayer, confession, fellowship, service and giving) have you seen an improvement in your understanding and practice since studying this book? Which of them do you still feel weak in? Discuss ways to improve in these areas.

Endnotes

Introduction

1. John Ortberg, "True (and False) Transformation," *Leadership*, 23, no. 3 (Summer 2002), 101.

2. I have been reading, studying and preaching for more than 40 years now. It is therefore practically impossible for me to separate original insights (of which there are very few) from what I have gleaned from the mind, heart and lives of others who are much further along in this journey of transformation into Christlikeness. The abundant use of quotations are ample testimony to that. Readers may well recognize my dependence on others in places I have not given any credit. I am almost certain, for example, that the four stages of Peter's conversion in chapter 1 did not originate with me, though the specific words to describe it are mostly mine—I think. I have no illusions about being the spiritual equivalent of a "self-made man."

3. Some readers might wonder why I have left out many important spiritual disciplines like fasting, solitude, secrecy and the like, and why I chose to address only these particular ones. There were two reasons, mainly. First, I have selected those disciplines that I have practiced long enough to be able to write with integrity and some degree of firsthand "field experience." Second, I chose the ones that in my judgment (flawed though it may be) were foundational and

which, I felt, were most accessible to people just getting started. Readers wanting to delve into the "missing disciplines" or take the ones I have included to a "higher" level have a wealth of material to draw upon from far more competent authors than I—Richard Foster and Dallas Willard, to name a couple.

4. George Barna, *The State of the Church: 2006* (Ventura, CA: The Barna Group, 2006), accessed online at www.barna.org.

Chapter 2

1. William Temple, Archbishop of Canterbury, as quoted in Warren W. Wiersbe, *The Bible Exposition Commentary: New Testament,* (Colorado Springs, CO: Cook Communications, 2001), 2: 190.

2. Robin Mark, "Lion of Judah" (Mobile, AL: Daybreak Music, Ltd., 1993).

3. Greg Gulley and Lenny LeBlanc, "No Higher Calling" (Nashville: Maranatha Music, 1989).

Chapter 3

1. Eugene H. Peterson, *Eat This Book: A Conversation in the Art of Spiritual Reading* (Grand Rapids, MI: Eerdmans, 2009), 17.

2. Phillip Keller, *A Shepherd Looks at Psalm 23* (Grand Rapids, MI: Zondervan, 2007), 73–74.

3. Eugene H. Peterson, *Take and Read* (Grand Rapids, MI: Eerdmans, 1996, 2000), 48.

4. Julian Green, diary entry, as quoted in Peterson, *Take and Read,* xi.

Chapter 4

1. Os Guinness and John Seel, *No God but God: Breaking With the Idols of Our Age* (Chicago: Moody, 1992), 18–19.

2. David F. Wells, *No Place for Truth* (Grand Rapids, MI: Eerdmans, 1993), 253.

3. Jerry Mander, *Four Arguments for the Elimination of Television* (New York: Harper Perennial, 1978), 197.

4. M. Scott Peck, *The Road Less Traveled* (New York: Simon and Shuster, 1985, 1978), 297.

5. Ibid., 300.

6. Ibid., 302–303.

7. Os Guinness, *God in the Dark: The Assurance of Faith Beyond a Shadow of Doubt* (Wheaton, IL: Crossway, 1996), 167.

8. Gordon MacDonald, *Ordering Your Private World* (Nashville: Thomas Nelson, 1985), 97.

9. Kathryn Koob, *Guest of the Revolution* (Nashville: Thomas Nelson, 1984).

Chapter 5

1. Arthur Bennett, *Valley of Vision: A Collection of Puritan Prayers and Devotions* (Carlisle, PA: Banner of Truth Trust, 1975), 28.

Chapter 6

1. Sewell Chan, "'I Apologize to the Public,'" *New York Times,* March 10, 2008, N.Y./Region section, online at http://cityroom.blogs.nytimes.com/2008/03/10/i-apologize-to-the-public/.

2. George Ridding, *The Southwell Litany* (Cincinnati, Forward Movement Publications, 1920). Online at http://www.resurrectionbeaches.org/SOUTHWELL%20LITANY1.pdf.

3. John White, *Eros Defiled* (Downers Grove, IL: InterVarsity Press, 1977), 45–46.

Chapter 7

1. Eugene H. Peterson, *Christ Plays in Ten Thousand Places: A Conversation in Spiritual Theology* (Grand Rapids, MI: Eerdmans, 2005), 226.

2. Gordon MacDonald, *Rebuilding Your Broken World* (Nashville, TN: Oliver-Nelson, 1988), 112–13.

Chapter 8

1. Elton Trueblood, as quoted in Roy B. Zuck, *The Speakers' Quote Book* (Grand Rapids, MI: Kregel, 1997), 118.

2. John Ortberg, *The Life You've Always Wanted: Spiritual Disciplines for Ordinary People* (Grand Rapids, MI: Zondervan, 2002), 120.

3. Ibid., 121.

4. Richard J. Foster, *Celebration of Discipline: The Path to Spiritual Growth* (San Francisco: Harper & Row, 1978), 130.

5. Ortberg, *The Life You've Always Wanted*, 121.

6. Dallas Willard, *The Spirit of the Disciplines: Understanding How God Changes Lives* (San Francisco: Harper & Row, 1988), 183.

7. Rick Warren, *The Purpose-Driven Life: What on Earth Am I Here For?* (Grand Rapids, MI: Zondervan, 2002), 258.

Chapter 10

1. Eugene H. Peterson, *Subversive Spirituality* (Grand Rapids, MI: Eerdmans, 1997), 134.

2. John G. Whittier, "Dear Lord and Father of Mankind," 1872.

3. Charles Colson, *Who Speaks for God?* (Wheaton, IL: Good News Publishers, 1985), 137, 139.

4. George Orwell, "Notes on the Way," from *The Collected Essays, Journalism and Letters of George Orwell,* ed. Sonia Orwell and Ian Angus (New York: Harcourt, Brace, and World, 1968), 2:15.